Hungry for Love

By Yvonne J. Douglas

Hungry for Love

By Yvonne J. Douglas

First published 2011 By Yvonne J. Douglas, Copyright ©.
TamaRe House Publishers

Revised edition Yvonne J Douglas 2013

This publication employs acid free paper and meets all ANSI standards for archival quality paper as well as meets all FSC standards for certification.

A CIP record of this publication is available from the British Library.

ISBN: 978-1491247679

HUNGRY FOR LOVE

Contents

Forward

By Gwenton Sloley

Sexual abuse is any sort of non-consensual sexual contact. Sexual abuse can happen to men or women of any age. Sexual abuse by a partner / intimate can include derogatory name calling, refusal to use contraception, deliberately causing unwanted physical pain during sex.

Yvonne shares from her own personal experiences as an abused child. Through both perspectives, the author walks the reader through the basics of each chapter, in order for the reader to apply what they have learned to their own life. Every chapter offers aftercare into the reality of healing from abuse, as well as being devoted to "taking the next steps."

Hungry for Love helps the survivor to realize their potential to move forward in their life. Yvonne shows through her own journey, whether or not one moves on is a personal choice. She encourages her readers to release the negativity that is within them and begin to focus on the positive things in life. Yvonne does not attempt to tell the reader that the memories will fade away and no longer surface. On the contrary, she confesses that she personally experiences the memories of her past; however, she chooses to let the memories go and move on with her life.

I applaud Yvonne Douglas for having the courage to be open about her experience many families have been destroyed once the lifelong secret of sexual abuse is out in the open with many often blaming them-selves for speaking out, to be left once again with the feeling of shame and guilt. So too often, people will not speak out about their past for fear of rejection across the world. I have recommended this book to many of my clients and their families as I have seen over the years in my job working with gang members on witness protection programme emotional trauma associated with abuse is likely to turn from one extreme to another.

This book, Hungry for Love, is a valuable resource in one's healing process from abuse. I believe it will inspire many survivors to finally be able to release the pains of their past. She writes in such a way that brings clarity to the reader and provides the optimism they need to grasp a hold of in order to move forward. I encourage all survivors of abuse to read this book and to cling to the tools written within the pages.

Gwenton Sloley

Author of Alone with my Thoughts

Acknowledgements

After 3 years of hard work my book has finally come together. It has not been an easy project due to all the emotions and memories that have arisen. However, it has been worth it. I am truly grateful to all who have supported, guided, inspired and advised me over the years of writing this book as well as life in general. I would like to thank my parents for giving me the genes of a determined young woman and for doing the best you could with the tools you had. Thank you granny for all you did for me and to my aunties and uncles. Thank you to my cousin Rockell and husband Randolph for your support and love. My children; thank you for your patience and unconditional love; for your acceptance and great sense of humour, I love you both dearly.

I give respect and a whole load of gratitude to the staff at the Priory in North London, in particular my therapist David. My very first therapist Rosemary for her love, patience and guidance, you do not realise how much you opened my eyes – thank you. Thank you to my friends who have always been there for me no matter what with your words of encouragement Nathalie, Lisa, Karen, Michelle, and Amanda-Jane. Natalie and Maria – you both supported and continued to have faith in me. Cheryl – God bless you. Lorna, yes I may well be famous! Elaine and Ronnie – love you both. Iona you planted the seed in me that I had the ability to write and publish, thank you. Karen I thank you for your words of encouragement and belief in me. Lorraine, my mentor and friend thank you, I did it. Angela, for many years you listened to me and to Paula; thank you both for listening. I hope your ears are still working. Carole thanks for your kindness and care. Rita; thanks not just for your help with my marketing of the book, but for being a friend too. Sandra, I'm so glad I met you – thanks. Thank you Christine for your support and remaining non-judgemental. To my old school friend Lana – I miss you.

Thanks to all the staff at Kairos – keep doing what you do. Thank you to those who have touched my life in a positive way and sorry I cannot mention every one of you, but you know who you are.

Thank you to all my siblings (I won't mention your names, to protect your identity). I love you all very much and despite it all we survived. Sean, thank you for your patience, and input and teaching me many important lessons. Rowan I thank you for all your hard work. Last but not least, I want to thank God and the Universe for giving me the courage, strength and determination for helping me along this journey and giving me the talents to write this book. I hope whoever reads this is truly inspired.

Note: most names have been changed to protect their identity.

Rowan Campus: Graphic designer

Gail Hill: Typeset designer

Prelude

In 2007 I finally melted and crashed; I could no longer hold it together and this time it felt permanent. I was married for the second time around had two lovely children, a comfortable home and a good job in the banking industry. Everything on the outside appeared to be normal, I was fairly happy, and was considered to be the so called life and soul of the party. Yes I was dealing with my emotions on and off, but was able to get rid of the downturns each time, with a few antidepressants, exercise, some counselling and self-help books, I was sorted.

Except, deep down inside something was still missing, like it always was; only I did not or could not admit it. It was like a gaping hole in the pit of my stomach. I felt I had done everything in my power to find a solution and now I had hit the wall running. Subconsciously, I tried to fill that gaping hole of emptiness with anything I could get my hands on; however it was now killing me – emotionally, mentally and physically.

I killed my emptiness firstly with food! And every diet I tried failed miserably. I could no longer cope nor fool myself any longer. The weight was ruining my life. I was having constant meltdowns, mishaps and relationship problems I was falling apart. How did I keep managing to get here again and again? Why was this still happening to me? I was so confused and nothing made sense anymore.

I needed answers and I needed them now, I became an addict of my own circumstances but even more distressing was that the addictions wasn't my primary problem – it was merely a symptom of something much bigger; and that immense problem was yet to be discovered. I realised that I did not have to go far to find the answers I was looking for, although I did have to go deep; deep within my very soul to find them. I suddenly found I was being railroaded on the most traumatic journey of my life...

This book is about a journey of self-discovery; a journey of rehabilitation and recovery to find an inner peace; a journey that would eventually find the missing pieces to fill that gaping hole that had been so empty for all of my life; a journey of fear, anger, loss and shame; leading to a journey of hope, fulfilment and love. This is my journey, my own personal story to share with you so that it brings you hope and inspiration.

Chapter 1

Early Beginnings – 1968 - 1973

My earliest childhood memories are quite patchy and the memories that always first come to mind when asked "tell me about your childhood" are ones of sadness, loneliness and neglect. I was born in 1968, a time when life was difficult for black people living in England. My mother was a single parent and I was her second child. My sister was one year old when I was born and we lived in a room in a house shared by other families. My mother, Nara was 19 when I was born and my father, Dougie 24; however they were not together when I entered into the world.

Both of my parents came from St Thomas in Jamaica – St Thomas is well known for its breadfruit. My mother was born in 1949 in Bath, famous for its natural hot running healing waters. She was the first born of her family and had six younger brothers and sisters. She did not get much of an education, frequently missing school in order to help out bringing up her siblings. Her parents came to England in the early 1950's leaving their children behind in Jamaica when my mother was about six years old. Nara and her siblings were scattered among aunties and uncles until their grandmother gathered them all together to live with her and their cousins in her home. My mother was sent for by her parents when she was 14.

It obviously took a while for Nara to settle in a foreign land, adjusting to a new life, re-bonding with her parents and becoming accustomed to having two other younger siblings who were born in England whom she had never met before, not to add missing her other siblings who were still in Jamaica eagerly awaiting the time for their departure to England.

Nara was a petite woman of 5 foot tall, very pretty with a honey brown skin tone. She was shy and very unassuming with a figure to die for. By the time Nara was 16 she met Dougie and became pregnant for him, she later gave birth to Charlene at the tender age of 17 two weeks before her 18th birthday. Dougie was seeing another woman at the same time, whom he later married leaving Nara with one child and another on the way. That other child was me and I was born a year later at the end of April and my half-sister Connie, whom he had with the other woman, was born two months after in June. You see Dougie was what you would call a 'ladies man'. He loved women and they certainly loved him. He was the kind of man that every woman wanted to be with: smooth, debonair, charming and well dressed; he was what you would call dark and handsome, without the tall, although he was not short!

Nara met David before I was born. David was 6 foot tall, very slender with an austere look about him. He later married Nara and they had four sons together, Jay, Alvin, Shane and Troy all born within one or one and half years of each other, Jay was born a year after me. Nara had had all of her 6 children by the time she was 25 years old. So here we all are Nara, David and six children living in a small house in Canning Town, East London.

As you walked through the front door of our house to your right was a small living room which was modestly furnished, with orange curtains. The fireplace had ornaments on top but no fire to keep us warm. As you walked past the living room there was a small dining room and through there the kitchen. The kitchen was a fair size and with a rather large sink. The house had no bathroom so we children had to bathe in the sink and once we were older we had to wash in a big metal bath. Sometimes when Nara wasn't around David had the job of bathing us. Charlene told me that we often cried due to the pain we felt in our private parts after bath times; something I cannot really remember. The toilet was outside the kitchen in a little lean to, which led onto the tiniest concrete garden with high fences, resembling something like a prison.

Upstairs were three small bedrooms, Charlene and I shared one bedroom, this was the smallest room of them all, I do not recall there being a door for our bedroom, Charlene and I shared a bed and we would cuddle up together to keep each other warm. I often recall being terrified in that bedroom; always thinking that someone was coming into our room. I frequently heard mice scratching away on a regular basis and this terrified me, causing my heart to beat at a rate far too fast for someone just trying to sleep peacefully. To the other side of the house upstairs was the room where my mother and David slept and adjoining was another room where my four brothers slept. Their room seemed a lot cosier than our room, although it only contained one large bed and a wardrobe.

We went to the local school Star Lane in Canning Town, which was less than five minutes away from our house. We regularly played out on the street, in those days it was safe to do so no matter how young you were. We would play out with the neighbours and have fun playing hopscotch, skipping, add and racing. I loved to play and had a very competitive streak in me. The ice cream man would frequently come down the street, but it was on the rare occasion that we were allowed to have any ice cream. One day David decided to treat the kids to an ice cream, I was excited readily looking forward to tasting the cold creamy substance that would delight my taste buds. David was outside buying the ice creams and he entered into the house with them, slowly he gave them out one by one. First to Jay, and he accepted gladly and started to lick frantically, then Alvin was handed his one, he took it and with his shy look slowly started to join Jay in enjoying their treat. I was becoming impatient, eagerly anticipating mine. He then gave Charlene hers and she took it willingly and licking it immediately at the same time giving me a wicked glance which said, 'I got mines first, and you ain't got yours". I started to feel a funny feeling in the pit of my stomach as I realised that there were more children than ice creams. At that point David simultaneously handed Shane and Troy their ice creams and they grabbed them out of his hands and started to lick profusely with big grins on their faces. I stood by in disbelief thinking: Where was my ice cream? Had he made a mistake? Could he not count? David then looked at me with a sinister grimace and it was then that I realised I wasn't getting one. This was another evil act that I had to encounter at the hands of this man. That lonely, desperate feeling of emptiness; one of rejection and shame engulfed me. This feeling was all too familiar with me and at this tender age of 5 was more than my little heart could bear. I didn't know where to put my face, as the other kids looked on not knowing whether to laugh at me or feel sorry for me. Neither of them offered me any of theirs and I was not consoled by any of them. I desperately needed to cry, but David hated it when we cried; 'Where was mummy?' I thought. 'I need my mummy.' This event I had not remembered for many years to come.

We had a little Yorkshire terrier whom we called Ashy. He was cute and fun to have around. We would play with him and he would chase us all into the kitchen, needless to say we made a lot of noise because we were having fun with our new pet. Mum could not cope with the noise and excitement this created so she got rid of Ashy; she gave him to the milkman. One day I came home from school and Ashy was nowhere to be seen. We all mourned for Ashy because we loved him very much and missed him dearly. Nara got rid of him because she could not afford to feed us let alone a dog. She was a full time stay at home mum and David often gambled instead of giving her housekeeping money!

Charlene and I spent some time with our biological father very occasionally and one day he took us to the fair at Wanstead Flats. It was a sunny day; I was 5 years old and very excited at the prospect of seeing my daddy and spending some time with him. He was so much nicer than David. We were on the swings, he stood below whilst we were up in the air going round in circles, it seemed like he was so far away. We waved frantically as we passed him every 20 seconds or so. He waved back smiling; he started waving goodbye and then all of a sudden he vanished into the air. Fear gripped me inside, my heart started to beat, that empty feeling engulfed me. Where was my daddy going? He was leaving us all alone in a fairground amongst strangers, anything could happen to us. The ride was no longer enjoyable; we started to cry hysterically for our daddy to return to us. By the time the ride came to an end my daddy had returned holding two large pink candyflosses in his hand. I was relieved and felt somewhat calm yet still agitated. He gave me this fluffy sweet stuff. It was pink and resembled cotton wool, it looked beautiful, but not edible, however, I did not need to be told more than once that I could eat this stuff and it relieved any feelings of agitation almost immediately.

Life at home was not much fun, especially now that Ashy had gone. Our family were poor; mum always seemed stressed, depressed or tired. She did not have much time for me. Mum sometimes left us alone in the house whilst she went out to do some part time work or to a party. I remember on one occasion all six of us were alone in the house, desperate for mummy to come home. We were scared and lonely and needed so much for someone to be there to take care of us and comfort us, but alas no one was home; we had to comfort each other somehow, some way. We had this particular ornament of a grey elephant with orange eyes and mysteriously one of its eyes had disappeared. We were terrified of this little elephant and believed that something creepy was going to happen to us instigated by this all powerful elephant with one orange eye. We became frenzied and sombre at the same time and Charlene ordered us all to sit on the sofa in a row. She started banging her head against the back of the sofa chanting "Mummy I want to come with you," mummy I want to come with you" repeatedly. Eventually we all started to join in following our big sister till we were in unison chanting simultaneously "Mummy we want to come with you," mummy we want to come with you," hoping with all our hearts that this chanting would bring our mum home to us speedily. The chanting helped calmed us down, in a way it felt like we escaped our scary world momentarily and felt safe for a while.

We were often left with David and this always made me uneasy, nervous and afraid as it was clear that he did not like me. I did not like him very much, he was mean to say the least and I found his behaviour towards me confusing. He singled me out amongst the others and treated me so unfairly. I was not allowed to sit around the dinner table with the rest of the family. I thought it might be because I did not know how to eat properly. There seemed to be no valid reason for this and it left me feeling ashamed and rejected as usual. I would sit on the sofa all by myself quietly eating my dinner. I was careful not to make a sound as I watched everybody else eating around the dinner table. I wanted so much to be a part of it, but alas I just was not good enough to sit with them all. My little heart felt so heavy and I frequently wondered why mummy wouldn't say nor do anything. What was wrong with her? David habitually teased me in front of the others; I would end up storming off wondering why he hated me so much. I had an intense fear of this man that lived in our house. Not only that, I soon developed a bad temper and was very stubborn, inside I felt so very sad, alone and empty, but I would never show just how much. I had to put on a brave face.

I developed a fondness for reading which I would use as a form of escape from my world, I always imagined myself as one of the characters in the book. I grew up thinking that I started reading so frequently out of choice, but I was later informed that I was told to go and read by my step-dad when he did not want to see or hear me. So I would go sit in a corner and just read and read and read. Despite the fact that I hated him for how he treated me; I still craved for him to like me and love me as his own. After all, isn't that what little girls need, to be loved and accepted by her primary caregivers? I also wanted my own dad to come and save me from this man, but he never did. 'Where was he anyway? Why does no-one love me? Why was life so unfair?' I often pondered.

Chapter 2

Tarnished – 1974

One day mum went out and left us with David, this always left me feeling scared. He had some friends come round and they all sat in the living room on the sofas talking and drinking whilst my brothers, sister and I played quietly in close proximity, waiting to be noticed. One particular man with very pale skin seemed very kind and Jay and Alvin sat on his lap whilst he spoke quietly to them. I became jealous and wanted to sit on his lap too, so I hung around waiting for my turn. In time, Jay jumped off his lap and ran into the dining room to play with the others; I was offered a place on his lap which I readily took.

I was happy to be sitting on his lap next to Alvin. Then all of a sudden, before I knew what was happening, this man slowly took his right hand and managed somehow to find its way to my fanny, instantly I froze, not knowing what to do. He started to move his finger around and with each movement, I became terrified, too shocked to even move. After a while, he got hold of my hand and placed it inside his trousers; it felt warm, clammy and horrid, yet still too scared to move and reveal what this man was doing I stayed. I was confused, I felt ashamed. I thought to myself, 'Can't they see what this man is doing? Why me? What did I do? This is awful! Surely this isn't right!' I could not handle this and as my mind wondered into another hemisphere full of pink fluffy candy floss, where nice things happen to little girls, the time drifted by. But before long reality kept creeping back and I was back in that living room with this nasty, ghastly devil doing nasty things to me. My mind went black, I felt that emptiness inside me quadruple in size and it was filled with all sorts of horrifying creatures all trying to hurt me. I needed to be brave. How do I get out of this?

Eventually with every little bone in my body I plucked up the courage to jump off this revolting creature and run towards the kitchen. I ran into the toilet and locked the door, I didn't want him to come and get me so I hid there for what seemed like eternity. I put my ear close to the door and listened to see if I could hear what was going on; all I could hear was my heart beating so hard I thought it would jump out. I finally conjured up enough courage to come out of the toilet; I slowly walked into the kitchen and proceeded to wash my hands. I could not stop washing my hands; I was at that sink, standing on a chair washing my hands forever. I felt dirty and needed to get that muck off and I thought the more I washed it the cleaner it would become and no-one would ever know that I touched his willy. Someone approached me, which startled me. I think it was my step-dad or even my granddad and he asked me "Why are you washing your hands like that for?" I did not know where to put my face or what to say so I just said "I don't know" rather sheepishly. I just wanted my mummy to come home, 'Where was she anyway?'

Mum finally arrived home and I told her exactly what had happened; how this ghastly man had done dirty things to me. Later that day the man came back to the house to impart sweets onto us; mum cussed him off our doorstep in true Jamaican style and told him never to show his face around our house again. Off he went with the sweets he intended to leave behind. Although I was upset that we would not be able to enjoy the sweets I was happy to hear that he was sent packing and I would never have to see him again. My mummy was amazing, I thought.

We lived in a council house on a fairly decent street; however it became too small and without a bathroom the house was no longer adequate for our large family so mum was trying to find us a bigger home to live in. She applied to the council for a larger home which would be more suitable, but the waiting list was long. It was not very often that a four bedroom property would come up even in those days. Mum became indignant one day and along with David and all six of us children stormed down to the local council office in order for them to listen to our plea of needing a larger home. Mum felt as if she was not being heard, so in order to make the staff listen they walked out of the building leaving all six of us with the strange looking people sitting behind the counter. Needless to say, we became terrified. 'Where was mummy? Why did she leave us here all alone? What did we do wrong? Who are these strange people?' We all started to cry nervously, and only the familiar face of our mother would settle us. After some time she returned to get us, we were ecstatic to see her return to collect us. It was not very long after that we were offered a huge five bedroom house in Forest Gate.

Chapter 3

New Home – 1975 - 1976

I do not remember leaving Star Lane, but I do remember arriving at Romford Road, the house was an old Victorian house with the highest ceilings you could imagine as a child. When we arrived we ran around the house quickly peeping into each room with excitement, never before had we seen so much space in one house and the garden was a dream come true for any child. There was a huge lawn in the middle of two concrete paths and beside each path was a flower bed. At the back of the garden was another large flower bed, this was paradise! As you walked through the doors of Romford Road there was a living room to your left with a fireplace, the hall way was long and a little further down next door to the cellar was a bedroom. There were four more steps and down them to your left a small dark kitchen and a conservatory which led out into the large garden. Straight ahead of the steps was a generous size dining room this also had a fireplace and a large window, the light in that room was glorious.

As you walked up the huge staircase you came to the bathroom on the left and further down the long hallway at the back of the house was a room which could have been used as a bedroom however, it looked like it use to be a kitchen because it had a sink in it, this later became the junk room, the room which housed items that had no real home. Next door to that room was a small bedroom but it was still a lot bigger than my old bedroom; however it was the coldest one in the house. Towards the front of the house upstairs was the master bedroom which was big enough to house four double beds and right next door to that room was another good sized bedroom which was larger than the one at the back of the house.

As I ran around the house with excitement wondering which room I would be sleeping in and imagining all the fun we would have in this beautiful large house I could not help but wish that my stepdad was not coming with us. The house seemed bare, we did not have much furniture to fill it with and it just seemed like we were moving into a mansion. I was six at the time and leaving Star Lane felt good, the house was so tiny, dingy and scary hopefully Romford Road would see happier times. Now that we had more space and a decent garden to play in mum would be happier, less stressed and have more time for us.

Our first night in the new house was chaotic; I assumed that I would be sleeping in one of the rooms with my sister. However the ogre ordered me to sleep in the cold back bedroom with Shane and Alvin, this was because we were the three that wet the bed. I was not happy with this decision; I wanted to be with my big sister so we could cuddle up and keep warm. I felt as if I was being banished to the cold small room with my younger brothers. 'Why was life so unfair?' Needless to say, I did wet the bed that night. I lost count of how many nights I had to spend in that room with my brothers but there did come a time, when we were more settled, that my sister joined me in that room and my brothers departed and slept in the room next to the master bedroom. So here we are in a five bedroom house using only three of them.

Life at Romford Road was a little better; however the presence of David sometimes made it hell. When he was at work we would play and be happy, Charlene and I would help take care of our brothers. We would play with them and keep them entertained, especially Troy, the youngest. He was so cute and we would play 'mamas and papas' with him, wrapping a red scarf round his head and pretending to send him off to the shops to buy groceries; he loved playing that game. As soon as David arrived home, we would suddenly be quiet finding somewhere to sit down so he would not be mad with us, it resembled something like musical chairs. Saturdays were unbearable, he was around all day although he would often pop out to the local betting office to place a bet and rush back home to watch the race. We would switch the TV over to watch cartoons when he went and as soon as we heard the key in the door we would have to turn it back over to racing. Saturdays were boring and tiresome. He would watch the races in such an animated fashion, shouting out at the horse he had just placed a bet on. For the Grand National he would chant "Go on Red Rum, go on Red Rum" – those words I can still hear in my distant memory today.

David detested children, who sucked their finger or wet their beds, and strangely enough Alvin, Shane and I were the three who sucked our tongue, thumb or finger respectively and were the ones who wet our beds very frequently. We were sadder than the others. Alvin and Shane were his second and third sons. There were times when David would do cruel things to stop Shane from sucking his thumb. One day he put hot pepper sauce on it. He even banged it with a hammer, when that happened we were all so very distraught and felt sorry for

Shane, but we dare not say anything for fear he may do something to us. We all sat in silence, glued to our chairs whist Shane cried profusely not able to be consoled. David had banged Jay's thumb with a hammer when he was a baby to stop him from sucking his thumb, and it worked. He would bite my finger (to this day I do not remember this, but was informed by a family member) to prevent me, but that never worked, sucking my finger soothed me, a comfort I needed because I was not getting it anywhere else.

Despite his cruel behaviour David still did fun things with his boys one of which was playing cricket. They would play in the garden using a real cricket ball, as it hit the bat it made a huge banging noise. One day whilst they were playing cricket I was in the garden doing my own thing as usual, quite happy in my own little world. My back was towards them and then all of a sudden I felt this awful pain, the ball had hit me on my back, I was bending down at the time and as I looked up the tears started to sting my eyes just as much as the ball had stung me. I looked around at everyone and no-one took responsibility for hitting me with the ball and there was no apology. Suddenly there was a roar of laughter coming from David as he looked on at me whilst the boys all stood there looking perplexed, not knowing whether to laugh along with their dad. I did not know what to do, the pain was excruciating and this grown monster was laughing at me, a little girl in distress. Confusion struck once more; questions ran through my mind 'Why is he laughing? Was it an accident? Did he do it? Did he do it on purpose? What did I ever do to this man? Where is my mummy?' I ran inside as quickly as my little legs could carry me, into my room and cried into my pillow.

One sunny day I was in the garden minding my own business digging up the dirt. I was again in my own little world and did not initially know that something was going on right in my vicinity. Then finally, I sensed someone standing over me, I swiftly looked up and there he was, my stepdad, grinning and standing over me dangling the biggest, ugliest looking worm he could find. I was petrified, my heart beating ten to the dozen, I got up as quickly as I could and ran inside screaming, leaving him and my brothers laughing at my expense. It seemed that David took delight in putting the fear of God in me, making me cry and seeing me miserable.

I was still wetting the bed and was often terrified by the time the sun rose in the morning, most mornings David would come into our room and pull the covers off us to check if I had wet myself and one awful morning he found that not only had I wet myself, I had also done a number two. He seemed to find this funny and he ran about the house waking everybody up, teasing and shouting that I had shit in the bed. I wanted the ground to swallow me whole so that I could escape living through this moment. I felt so ashamed, dirty and mortified. Why had I not got up to go to the toilet? I know why, I was scared. I was forever scared. Scared to get up; scared to move; scared to breath. The evil taunts of this man were deafening, I wanted to be somewhere else, in a fairy tale land for little girls only.

We often ran out of essentials, like bread, sugar and biscuits, so mum would send Charlene and me to the local shop which was two minutes away. We liked going to the shop because more often than not there was always change left over and we would buy ourselves sweets with it. We saw it as our little treat; after all we were the older ones with responsibility. Food did not last long in our house, there were so many mouths to feed and there never seemed to be enough money even though David worked at Fords in Dagenham. Sometimes all we had to eat was bread and butter however; we were very innovative and would put sugar or condensed milk into the bread thus making it more desirable to eat. We would wrap our little tongues around the bread with our eyes all glazed over making humming noises. In fact, we would do this whether there was enough food in the house or not, it was delicious.

Mum and David frequently argued and there were times that David would hit mum. One occasion he was so enraged that he picked up a dining room chair, it was made of light veneer wood and had sky blue seats, he picked it up as if to throw it at her, we were petrified and confused. Not knowing what to do, we all ran out into the garden hysterically. Outside we wondered what would be the fate of our mother and whether he would start attacking us. We huddled together for much needed comfort and security. When we finally went back inside the chair was in pieces, so was mum. Mum often spent a lot of time just lying in bed ill, Charlene and I would look after her and bring her food. We often heard her crying behind the door, this unsettled and troubled us deeply.

We attended the Local Kingdom Hall which was 20 minutes walk from our home. The meetings were often boring and Alvin would nearly always sleep throughout the meetings and sometimes all the boys would fall asleep; it was a job waking them up when it was time to go home. We sometimes got a lift home from brothers who had empty cars but not always as there were so many of us. We had some good friends there who looked out for us. One night when David was working the night shift two of the elders came to our home and before we knew it, they were helping us pack black bags with our belongings. They helped get us all ready, snuck us out of the house and drove us and mum to a local woman's refuge. It seemed that my mum had enough of the beatings and needed to get away from that cruel man. I was eight years old when this happened and as usual I was confused and excited at the same time. Although it was all a bit of a shock to me I was ecstatic to be away from that man, but not from our lovely house.

Life at the refuge was not very pleasant to say the least, there were different families living in this converted house. A Greek, West Indian, Irish and an English family. It was oversubscribed and because of our desperate situation they managed to squeeze us in. We had to sleep on blue garden loungers because there were not enough beds. It was not a very hygienic place and we had to share a bathroom and having to use it made me wish I was back at home in our mansion. I felt like a fish out of water there, everyone seemed so volatile and angry, even the kids. I was trying to figure out what was going on and make sense of the situation. At times it felt like an exciting adventure and then it felt a bit like a scary movie. We made friends with Barbara and her children, they were another black family. Barbara's children were slightly older than us but they took care of us, showed us the ropes and played with us. Many an evening was spent playing monopoly, which at times became extremely boring. We eventually managed to settle down and get use to our new surroundings.

After a few months, we were able to return home. The prospect was exciting, but I was sad to leave our new friends behind, they had become our extended family. I cried as I said my goodbyes although we were to stay in touch. The journey seemed lengthy and I was becoming impatient, I could not wait to be home in my own bed. Even though I was told that David would not be there, I still felt a little apprehensive and prayed hard that he definitely would not be there. "Please Jehovah, make him not be there, so that we can live happily ever after," I prayed quietly to myself. When we arrived home, there was an awful smell in the house which made me want to heave; it seemed like it had not been cleaned for ages and the toilet needed flushing. I searched the house high and low to ensure that David was not there, thankfully there was no sign of him. I felt a relief that made my whole body feel like it had never felt before. I was able to exhale and be free to enjoy what was left of my childhood, so I thought.

Chapter 4

No more evil Stepdad – 1977 - 1978

Life without David was definitely a lot better and very different. Everyone seemed more relaxed and somewhat happier. However, I still felt this emptiness inside me which I could not understand. My mother was sad although also relieved that he had gone, she became lonely so she arranged for Charlene and I to move into her bedroom. It was huge so there was no issue with space. She brought two single beds on hire purchase from Jeffrey's and Sons and we shared the room with our mum. We felt privileged we would spend lots of time talking, mum would share her problems with us, it made me feel all grown up.

Our grandmother, whom we called Granny (my mother's mum), became very much a part of our life. She was shorter than mum and was round and cuddly looking, her hair thick, black and long. I remember her having a faint moustache. Although she was not what you would call a warm person, she was there for us. She helped us out a great deal. She worked very hard looking after our granddad; he was a very miserable and an awfully quiet person, he would just sit in his dining room smoking his pipe and watching TV looking quite creepy. Charlene and I would visit them in Manor Park every Saturday.

We were nine and ten, old enough to travel that far by ourselves now and the very first time we ventured out we were excited that we were now old enough to make this journey. We felt grown up and responsible. We skipped along Shrewsbury

Road feeling happy and confident; we then arrived at Shelley Avenue and thought how easy it was. However, after some time we could not find the house. We became worried, we were certain this was the right road, we even recognised the trees. We turned onto High St North and became even more confused until we ended up at Manor Park Broadway, 10 minutes from home. The realisation set in, we were lost and ended up doing a full circle finishing right where we started. The adults found it quite funny, although Charlene and I did not, we were disappointed because we had to wait for the following Saturday before we could try going again.

On our visits to granny she taught us how to sew, bake, and iron. We would also help her vacuum her house. We did not mind helping too much, although we thought it unfair that we had to clean and vacuum when she had two big kids there who only seemed to argue constantly. It was no surprise that they argued so nastily because they were only copying what they saw, granny and granddad were always at each other's throats. Charlene and I just sat and watched quietly, silently frightened due to all that we had witnessed in our own home. Still trips to granny were good because we never went home empty handed – cakes and pastries always accompanied us home. My sweet tooth was developing nicely.

I was always a chubby girl, more so than Charlene, but it was not something that bothered me. I liked my food, especially sweets and chocolate, mars bars, marathons, dime bars, topics, rhubarb and custard sweets, pineapple chunks, tootie fruties were amongst my favourites but cakes were always at the top of my list. Granny's cakes were the best; she made carrot cake, West Indian black cake, Madeira cake and she taught us how to bake. Charlene and I would test our culinary skills at home and we even made sweet potato pudding (which, of course, granny taught us how to bake). A week would not go by when we did not bake.

Chapter 5

School

School was fine, when we moved we ended up going to Sandringham Primary which was about a 10 minute walk from home, although it seemed longer walking along the busy Romford Road each morning. I had joined that school from the infants and again I do not remember much about the infants, although there was an occasion when I was being naughty, it was bad enough for me to get a good hiding from the head teacher – Mr Howl was tall and had dark hair, he was quite handsome, if you like that sort of thing, and menacing looking at the same time. He took me out of the classroom and walloped me on the palm of my little hand with his large man's hands. I looked up at him with sorrowful eyes and cried; I convinced myself that I deserved it because I had a temper on me and a very stubborn streak.

By the time I moved up to the juniors to accompany my sister I felt like a big girl now. I was very fond of my teacher Miss Passmore, she was quite firm but she seemed so loving and caring and I wanted to be her favourite student. I loved it when she would read us stories; I would often drift off into my own world. Because we were Jehovah's Witnesses we were not allowed to go into the assemblies in the mornings, so Charlene and I along with other Witness children were excused from the assemblies and would deliver the milk to each classroom. This was no easy task; it took two of us to carry one crate to each classroom. Nevertheless we got on with it and enjoyed our roles as milkmen.

The following year I had Mr Lichmore as my teacher, a tall black man who reminded me of my father, although not as good looking. However, I became attached to him because he could have been the father that I did not have around at the time. I would often walk around the playground with him whenever he was on playground duty and I felt special. I had a crush on Paul a white boy who had an older brother in my sister's year. They were always very well dressed and looked like twins. I was attached to him and I always felt excited when he was ever in my group or when we played together. However, he did not stay at the school because they moved away which left me feeling quite alone abandoned and empty.

My biological father was by now living in New York with his new family. He would call me and Charlene on the phone, write us letters and send some money. When the letters came we were always excited, receiving the money was always a treat. We would have to get the dollars converted into sterling, which sometimes caused an inconvenience. However, we would use the money to buy ourselves a new outfit and maybe, no definitely, some sweets too. How I wished that my daddy was here with us in England.

One Saturday morning we received a message from our other grandma telling us to come over to her house in Stratford. She did not have that much to do with us until this time. When we arrived my dad with his other family were here on holiday. I was overwhelmed and excited to see them, with their American accents. Here he was, the man of my dreams standing before me, my very own daddy. How handsome he looked and very well dressed. His wife was in tow, bloody hell (I was not allowed to swear) I thought, 'She is not as pretty as my mum.' My sister Connie who was the same age as me and about the same height with her hair long enough for pony tails and her shy smile. Dirk – a year younger wearing shorts and looking like a little tyrant and my baby sister Sandra who was about 18 months and ever so cute. Then there was Marcia their older half-sister whose accent was a mix between Jamaican and American.

My grandma had a big house, she had lodgers staying in her other bedrooms, which meant all of us sharing only two bedrooms – we spent a lot of time with them and even slept over on weekends, every moment was precious. Five of us shared one single bed, it was a very tight squeeze but we managed it somehow, although occasionally one of us would fall off in the middle of the night. We did not mind sharing the bed; we just enjoyed being together and having a laugh.

I remember the day when my dad came to my school for parents evening. He turned up wearing a cream suit, a bowler hat, sunglasses and his gold chains and rings. My daddy always dressed to impress, I guess he was what you would call a poser, and as he strode along through the playground I felt really proud to be his daughter. Classmates ran up to me excitedly asking, "Is that your dad?" and I would proudly say with the biggest smile on my face "Yes, that's my dad."

We couldn't spend every night there due to school and one day Charlene and I were told to come over to grandmas earlier than usual. When we arrived there I could feel a different atmosphere in the house, and all the suitcases were visible, it was evident that they were leaving to go back to New York. I was completely and utterly devastated when I realised this. My daddy was leaving me again and taking away my new brothers and sisters whom I had bonded with. The feeling of abandonment and emptiness swept over me once again. The tears I cried were insurmountable; I was already missing them before they had even departed. My dad had bought my sister and me many gifts for us to take home, a school bag, some clothes, shoes, a watch which was great, but it was not what I really wanted, I just wanted them all to stay. 'Why was life so unfair? Doesn't my daddy love me?' I cannot remember how I dealt with their departure over the next few weeks; the food was my comfort as usual.

My next teacher in primary school was Ms Yates, I did not take to her, she was a thin woman, she wore glasses and behind them her eyes seemed beady and cold. Ms Yates was very strict and I was often in trouble with her. I remember playing in the Wendy House, I loved it. There were so many toys, dolls, clothes and shoes that we could dress up in. We loved playing mothers and fathers. Playing mum was good, because it made me feel all grown up where I was in control!

I had a close friend her name was Deborah, her mum owned the hairdressers on Katherine Road and they lived in the flat above. I was allowed to go visit Deborah at her house occasionally and I enjoyed those visits because there weren't many people in her family, so it was always quiet and I had Deborah to myself. Her flat was always very clean and tidy, albeit our house was clean but very rarely tidy, how could it be with six children? Deborah was a nice friend and she would always offer me a drink and biscuits or sandwiches when I went to see her. As usual I felt quite attached to her, so when

Deborah told me one day that they were leaving London I was naturally very upset. I withdrew for a while and found Deborah's departure difficult to deal with and resorted to my usual comfort of food. I had stopped sucking my finger by now, I used stop and grow nail varnish on it for a while. It tasted nasty and it helped me to stop. Even though I loved sucking my finger, I was too big to still be doing it.

In my final year of primary school I was fortunate enough to have Miss Passmore as my teacher again. I was very happy although she had remarried and she was now Mrs Edwards. Again, listening to her tell stories was always enchanting. We would sit on a mat near her all in a circle and listen intently to her story telling. She was brilliant at it and I always made sure that I got to sit right next to her. My favourite stories that she read were 'Tom's Midnight Garden,' I always imagined myself being in that secret garden, and then 'The Lion, The Witch and The Wardrobe' – I was hooked on that story, and just wanted to go through that wardrobe never to return to my world, my reality again. Even though evil stepfather was no longer around to make fun of me and treat me cruelly, the damage was already done, I did not really like myself and I was still very fearful of people and wanted so much for everybody to like me, I was very sad on the inside and the empty lonely feeling always seemed to be there.

Nevertheless, I was very good at pretending that I was ok when in fact I was not. I developed the knack of making jokes, making people laugh and portraying this bubbly happy person. This helped in my quest to get everyone to like me. I was good at performing and one of our class plays was about teeth where chubby Robert and I were the dentists whilst everyone else in the class were teeth. We made costumes that the teeth could wear and Robert and I wore white aprons. We had to explain what each tooth was for and it was done in a very professional manner. I enjoyed taking part in the play and I performed to the best of my ability. So when at the end of term there were auditions for the school play I earnestly went along.

The play was Aladdin and I went along hoping to get the part of the princess, I was very excited sitting down waiting for Mrs Edwards (who was in charge of the school play) to call out our names for the parts we had auditioned for. When it was time for her to choose the part of Princess I sat there as tense as ever just waiting for my name to be called. My name was not called for the part of the princess and I was visibly upset, I thought to myself, 'That's just typical, I never get what I want, and she's probably going to use me as a prop now. She said I was brilliant in the class play, so why didn't she choose me.' By this time most of the parts had already gone, there was only Aladdin's mother and Aladdin left to be picked. Aladdin's mother was picked, Michael was chosen to play the part; this made no sense to me. By now I was inwardly seething with all sorts of negative messages flying around in my head. I was not going to be in the school play, I had dreamt of being in that play and now it was to no avail. Mrs Edwards had praised me about how good I was in the class play, so why was she ignoring my talents now? But to my surprise, my name was called out to be Aladdin. I could not believe what I was hearing, "Yvonne I want you to play Aladdin, after such a wonderful performance in the class play you just have to be the star of this play." Well I was gobsmacked and ecstatic, 'Me Aladdin?! At last something good is happening in my life,' I thought.

Rehearsals were fun; we had to miss quite a few lessons in order to perfect our roles in the play. Our costumes were great, at first I had to wear rags but later on in the play I had to wear an amazing lilac two piece suit with silver bits in it, and some sort of turban. Everything about the play was just brilliant, from the costumes to the scenery and performing for so many people. We had to perform to the school, to the parents during one lunch time and again to the parents one evening. My mother came to see me perform and I wanted to do my very best so that she would be proud of me. It was probably the most fun I had had in my little life so far. When we were applauded at the end the sound of the applause resonated within me, I felt alive and special and my adrenaline was swishing all over my body. I received so much praise from the teachers and parents afterwards about how well I had performed and it was then that I realised I wanted to become an actor. My mother said I did well but she did not seem to be overly proud like I wanted her to be, and I certainly was not encouraged to pursue acting. In fact I was discouraged.

Mum took on a lodger, her name was Leanne and she came from Kent. She was pretty and slim with long brown hair and blue eyes. She stayed in the room downstairs next to the cellar. We loved having her around, every Friday she would buy six fudge bars and throw them up in the air for us all to catch. We all scrambled around making sure that we would get one, the thing is there was really no need because there was always enough for each of us, nevertheless, it was fun.

Mum was seeing one of the brothers from the Kingdom Hall; his name was Rick, a white man with brown hair, very tall with a chiselled face and quite handsome, again, if you like that sort of thing. He seemed very weird and their courtship did not last very long because as it happened he started seeing Leanne behind mum's back and when they were caught his excuse was 'Too many children.' Leanne had to leave the house which was quite sad because we became very fond of her, but could not believe that she would betray our mother like this. Mum met many brothers who liked her very much, and after all why wouldn't they she was very attractive, slim and still quite young despite the fact that she had six children. But each time they would all pull away with the same excuse for not taking it further – 'Too many kids.' I felt sorry for mum, but she always seemed to attract the men that did not want to commit to her.

Chapter 6

Teenage Years – 1979 - 1984

Moving onto secondary school was quite traumatic for me; luckily Charlene was already a student at Forest Gate Secondary School. However walking into such a large arena of different buildings was quite daunting. My close friends from primary school went to other schools – Dionne went to St Angela's, Karen went to Stratford and so did Nevrez. I felt somewhat alone going to Forest Gate, wondering if I would be able to make new friends; not yet convinced of my ability to do this. There were others from Sandringham going to Forest Gate, but I was not particularly close to them. I just had to get on with it I thought.

There were some real characters at Forest Gate that stood out. Timothy just seemed to be constantly angry and I feared him terribly. Susan who was very loud and confident, but also quite aggressive, I also feared her somewhat. Pamela from Guyana, who joined our year a bit later on, she was different from everyone else, and seemed a little wild in my eyes, maybe it was because she was teased a lot and stuck up for herself. Then there was Lara, tall dark skinned Indian and Black mix with long curly shiny hair and pretty – the envy of most girls in the year. She later became my best friend.

The form class that I was assigned to was 1G which meant I was in the Grosvenor house. Lara, Asha, Baljinda and Julie were the girls I hung around with. We were a good team, a mixture of different personalities and cultures. Lara was the leader and we all followed. I looked up to her quite a bit and wanted to be as bright, pretty and as slim as her, but that was not to be. Instead I was her short, chubby, not so bright side kick.

I spent many afternoons at Lara's home after school always to return home to my seemingly miserable mother who always wanted me straight home after school and did not want us bringing our school friends home with us. So I would go to Lara's house where I was very welcome by her parents. Her mother often said that I was like a daughter to her. Even her dad was very friendly and welcomed me into their home. They seemed to really like me which made me want to visit them as often as I could. They had a dog which was kept on a lead most of the time and I often had to pass him to go upstairs, he would always bark viciously every time I passed. I could not understand why he would not get use to my scent, I was petrified of this dog they called Max. He was an ex-police dog, very aggressive and they had to eventually put him down at Battersea dogs home, because he could not be retrained. Lara was very upset, I went along and comforted her, although deep down was quite pleased as it meant I would not have to be scared going to Lara's home anymore.

I found school quite difficult at times, especially maths. It seemed to take forever for me to grasp the concepts of algebra, trigonometry and the like. But once the penny dropped I found it manageable. However, maths always seemed to get me into a panic. English Literature and Language were subjects that I loved and I flourished in those subjects. I also enjoyed Physics although it could have been due to the fact that I was the teacher's pet. Taking part in class plays was always fun, however, drama classes were very minimal. I wanted to pursue drama and become an actor, remembering fondly my Aladdin days. However, I was discouraged from doing this because 'It was not a profession that a Christian should pursue'; I was told by the elders of the Jehovah's Witness faith. I could not understand how they came to that conclusion, because all I knew was that there was a fire in my bones that drew me to wanting to act for a living.

I often felt out of place at school and always felt like I needed the protection of Lara. On one occasion I had an argument with Coreen. It started out so trivial and escalated to the point where we were going to have to fight it out in the dry play area at lunch time. I already had one fight before with Michael in my first year of secondary school, and remembering the fear of the fight and having to face the headmistress, I was not looking forward to it. Everyone around goaded us and wanted to see some action. I had to represent and Lara coached me on how to put up a good fight. Firstly, I had to call her 'A fucked up piece of grey meat.' 'But I don't swear Lara, it's forbidden,' I thought. But a part of me wanted to say it, because then maybe people would start to respect me. Using the 'F' word started to feel appealing and I thought, 'What the heck' and blurted it out "You fucked up piece of grey meat." I started to feel like one of the tough girls now and my adrenaline rushed through my body like a whirl wind. My heart was beating like a drum and my fingers flickering with nerves. I was scared and excited at the same time as I approached Coreen and finally I was off landing a firm punch in her face. 'Was this really me being so violent? Was I really capable of such brutality? Oh bloody hell, yes I was!' I started to enjoy it as

I continued to lash out hardly allowing Coreen to get a good hit at me even though she tried. 'Wow, I am tough, I can stick up for myself, I am somebody;' all these thoughts were going around in my head and I continued to thump her. The fight ended with me being dragged off her before I did any real damage. I started to compose myself and levelled out my breathing whilst fixing my clothes back into place. I won the fight hands down and felt very proud of myself because initially I did not think I had it in me. It certainly gave me some much needed confidence. Some of the other children who preferred Coreen to me were not happy that I had won and one of them even kicked me in all the commotion afterwards. I did not care because I came out victorious. I won!

Some of the black boys in my year were dating a few of the white girls and us black girls had issues with that. I couldn't help but think that I was so undesirable in their eyes. This was another thing that added to me feeling insecure within myself, I dealt with this by picking on one of the girls by intimidating her whenever she walked by. This gave me a misplaced feeling of self-worth and power.

During my time at Forest Gate I had crushes on several boys in my year. Unfortunately for me the boys I liked did not like me and it made me feel so unlovable, ugly and fat. I so wanted someone to like me, the way Godwin loved Lara. Godwin was 2 years older and he and Lara went out for a good few years, even until after we left school in 1984. I often played gooseberry with them and although I was jealous that Lara had a boyfriend and I did not I still thought that Lara was way too pretty for Godwin. I told Charlene what I thought and she in turn told Lara's sister and it eventually reached Lara's ears. Lara confronted me about this and I found it so difficult to justify what I said and it made me feel so bad for expressing an opinion.

In the third year of secondary school a sleek looking Asian boy joined Forest Gate by the name of Ajaz. He was not like your normal Asian boy. He was flash and loud and quite a bad boy. He often played around with me and my crew and ended up asking me out. I was so afraid by this proposal because I was not expecting it and as much as I wanted a boyfriend I was not allowed to go out with boys. But temptation got the better of me and I said yes. 'At last someone likes me. I am pretty after all. Hold on a minute, what does he see in me? Why me? What does he want from me?' I was confused yet again. So here I was with my first boyfriend. My nerves would get the better of me and I found being alone with him very difficult so I strategically managed to stop us being unaccompanied too often (the elders would be proud of me). When we were on our own we would just walk around the small streets surrounding the school.

One occasion he took me to a very quiet area near some flats, we held hands as we walked and eventually we stopped at a very secluded area. He got close to me and my heart started beating way too fast plus my palms were sweating. He put his arms around my waist and at first it was nice to be held like that but suddenly I started to panic thinking 'What the hell is going on here? What does he want from me? Yuk yuk yuk!' I had a notion that he wanted to kiss me, and I immediately froze. I was right and he started to bring his lips closer and closer to mine, I had to distract him somehow, so I carried on talking. I could not kiss him even if I wanted to; again confusion got the better of me. 'He's so good looking, I do fancy him, I feel sick, I feel scared, but he is so gorgeous I feel nervous, no I can't, yes I can, no, no, no.' I couldn't and didn't kiss him.

Charlene somehow found out that I was seeing Ajaz and told mother. I was reprimanded and told that I would have to end the relationship immediately. I knew very well that boyfriends were not allowed. I was very upset and hated my sister for having such a big mouth and trying to spoil my fun. I plucked up the courage and told Ajaz that I had to end the relationship and he was none too pleased and still wanted to carry on in secret, to which I agreed even though I knew it was wrong. However, after more failed attempts of trying to kiss me he finally gave up and went out with some other chubby girl instead. He told me "If you won't kiss me then I will go out with someone who will." Those words stung and I felt that he only wanted me for one thing and what with my sister and mother on my back I just left well alone. I once again felt that life was not fair and feeling despondent I turned to my comfort of food.

Christmas at school was always miserable for me, as Jehovah's Witnesses we did not celebrate Christmas, Birthdays or Easter. We were not allowed to take part in the activities at school – I would have to make plain cards when everyone else made Christmas cards. When it was time for the Christmas party I had to go home. Many people gave me Christmas cards and I felt bad that I was not allowed to reciprocate. Some of the children could not understand my reasons for not celebrating and even though I could understand I still felt it was unfair. I just felt like I did not belong, like a spare part, not participating. The boys at school would become quite excited around Christmas and bought mistletoe from the local flower shop and would hold it over their heads and go around looking for girls to kiss. I knew I should not get involved but I thought 'What the hell!' and allowed persistent Gary a kiss, I moved towards him to kiss him on his cheek but before I could get to his cheek he swiftly turned round and managed to plonk his lips on mine. I was not amused! Gary use to chase me and other girls in primary school in order to feel our budding breasts and gage our sizes – apparently, according to Gary I was half a handful at the time. 'Bleeding cheek,' I thought.

We were entitled to free school meals as mum was a full time stay at home mother. I did not mind having school dinners especially when the desserts were sticky toffee pudding, apple crumble, spotty dick and coconut sponge all with custard. But when they gave us desserts like tapioca pudding and semolina and jam I was very upset because those desserts were just not worth having, although I would still have the semolina but could not stomach the tapioca – disgusting tiny balls in a watery milky mixture. Whenever the dinner ladies would shout out if anyone wanted seconds I would always rush up for more food. In fact I would often make sure I was at the end of the dinner queue so that I would be one of the last to finish my dinner and be around for second helpings. As soon as I finished my dinner I would then walk to Lara's house, she lived about 10 minutes from the school and always went home for dinners. So I would go and pick her up. Even though I enjoyed my school meals I was jealous that Lara went home for lunch. Lara's mother was often home as she worked two minutes from their home and she would also go home for lunch and when her dad worked the night shift he would sometimes be there also. From Lara's house we would sometimes go and pick up Asha if we had enough time, she also went home for lunch; all my close friends went home for lunch except me, I felt left out. Baljinda and Julie always came back to school in the afternoon with sweets and Baljinda was quite generous with her sweets unlike Julie. Army and Navy, cola cubes, pineapple chunks were the favourites even though they would cut the top of our gums.

At times I would be overwhelmed and just start crying for what appeared to be nothing. Lara and Asha would always be there to console me and wanted to know what was wrong, but I did not know myself why I was crying, nor could I explain what was wrong. I did know that I felt very sad and lonely, but I dare not tell them that.

Chapter 7

Extended Family

My favourite aunties were Gean and Vern. They were quite funny and Charlene and I would occasionally spend weekends with them. It was easy to get to their house, one straight bus towards Ilford on the Romford Road. We had to walk under a bridge which was a little scary for us due to the darkness and the narrow pavements, but we always got through ok. The journey time seemed to take forever despite it being an easy one. They lived in a little flat above the Kingdom Hall in Ilford. I enjoyed visiting them, although I did not like their pokey little kitchen. In fact everywhere in that flat was very tiny apart from maybe the living room, and it was quite clear that it was too small for the both of them, however, they seemed happy enough living there. Besides they were both under 5 foot tall so they were well suited to the flat. They did not spend much time there because they both worked part time as secretaries and the rest of the time they spent as pioneers. Pioneers were people who spent most of their time preaching and conducting bible studies with people who showed interest in the Jehovah's Witness religion. They took this very seriously and it was because they were so good at it and dedicated that they were able to rent the flat above the Kingdom Hall.

They ate quite healthily; breakfast was muesli and yogurt which I did not mind trying as I looked up to them and tried to fashion myself after them, they seemed so posh compared to my mother. Dinner would often be chilli con carne and rice. Not many desserts there, although Gean baked occasionally. Whenever Charlene and I stayed over we would always have to go preaching with them. Sometimes it was good when they had bible studies, which meant we would be invited into people's warm house and offered tea, and if we were lucky, biscuits would accompany the tea. I would perhaps have a couple of those biscuits as I did not want to appear to be greedy and as I often copied what my aunties did I would stop at one or two. However, I had this battle in my head with the biscuits that were sitting on the plate, my head kept telling me to have another and another and I could not focus on the bible study. Often times preaching was boring and I wished we could just stay at home and chill at times. There would be times that we would be out all day Saturday which was difficult to handle, I was often very hungry and it seemed that my aunties could go for hours and hours without having to eat, this was foreign to me and I would just suffer in silence.

There came a time when Gean and Vern decided to move all the way to North London. Apparently pioneers were much needed in that part of London. So they packed up and left. That was a sad time because they lived much further away; I did not see them as often, although Charlene and I would occasionally make the trip on the tube to go and see them. Eventually Gean decided to come back to East London. She could not settle and was missing the rest of the family. So she left Vern, which was remarkable because wherever you saw Vern you saw Gean, they were quite inseparable.

On her return to East London Gean lived with us for quite some time and I enjoyed having her live with us. I looked up to my aunty Gean, she looked very much like my mother but she seemed happier and she had the time to talk to me about almost anything. She seemed to know everything and I valued our relationship, she was only about 13 years older than me and we had fun together. I would call her 'Miss Know All.' Charlene loved to tease, it seemed like that was her purpose in life as we were growing up. She would tease aunty Gean a great deal and always thought whatever she did was funny, although at times it was not.

In fact, Charlene also teased me immensely and she enjoyed every minute of it. Certain things would make my nerves feel on edge which made it feel like insects were crawling all over my body causing me to itch like crazy; in fact Charlene suffered from this more so than I did, it ran in the family. But whenever Charlene found something that would make me feel like that she would try to recreate such things and show them to me thus prolonging my itchy state. On one occasion I felt like I was going off my head and I had to get away and lie down in order to calm my nerves. The peace and quiet was all that I needed to feel normal again. Charlene took great delight in causing me this much distress.

Charlene would borrow my clothes without asking and thought nothing of it. On the other hand, if I wanted to borrow Charlene's clothes I would always ask and was always refused. I would complain to my mother about this but nothing was ever done. It became so bad that I would become very angry and in the middle of my tantrums claim that Charlene was mum's favourite; it seemed obvious to me that this was the case. Charlene seemed to get away with so much more than I did.

I remember when I was about seven Charlene told me to put my mouth over the spout of a metal tea pot and pull upwards with my mouth. At first I said "No," however, she somehow managed to convince me that nothing would happen to me; she said that she had already done it and nothing horrible happened to her. I felt reassured by my older sister and believed her and did just as she said even though I could not see the point of the exercise. I approached the teapot slowly and very carefully put my mouth over the spout, it was warm and then I slowly pulled upwards as I took a deep breath. And before I knew it my mouth was on fire as I sputtered the liquid out. Needless to say my mouth was scalded. I started crying. Charlene was laughing and running away as I tried to catch her. 'How horrid of her,' I thought.

Charlene and I were pretty overweight by now; our sweet tooth was nicely developed. Granny was always trying to lose weight and was a regular member of weight watchers and slimming world. She took Charlene and me to weight watchers. My first experience of this was that of humiliation, here I was a young teenage girl having to go to a place like this to try and lose some weight. How did it get this far? Weight watchers did not really work, I would follow the plan to the best of my ability and each week I would not lose much weight, there were weeks when I would put on and would be very tempted to punch the woman who weighed me because I was convinced that she was either lying or she had dud scales. It was so disheartening and demoralising for me.

One year granny took Charlene, Jay and I to the Isle of Wight on a Pontins holiday. We were extremely excited; it was our very first holiday. All I can remember about that holiday was the geese that chased us, and being terribly afraid of them. The gambling arcade, where we lost quite a bit of our £10 spending money; became frustrated and angry with each other because of it. Being forced to enter the lovely legs competition which I did not win and knew I would not win because my legs were bandy. The disco dancing competition I won for my age group. I was over the moon about it. I felt special, being recognised again for my talent just like when I played Aladdin. They took my picture and there was an article about it in the local Newham Recorder some weeks later. Then there was Shane, one of the Blue Coats on the holiday, he had blonde hair and he was so nice to us, just doing his job presumably. However, it did not take long before I developed a full blown crush on the man. I was besotted and would look for him everywhere, I was convinced that I loved this man; I was only 14 at the time. When it was time to leave for home, I was completely and utterly devastated and cried many tears and wouldn't talk much for days.

Some weeks after the holiday, the article appeared in the local newspaper about me winning the dancing competition. I felt proud and the kids at school could not believe that this was the Jehovah's Witness Yvonne that they knew. I was due to be baptised in the summer. When the elders found out about the article I was summoned and told that I would not be allowed to get baptised this time round because it was not fitting for a Christian to be seen taking part in disco dancing. I could not believe what they were saying and was very upset by their decision, feeling that they were being a little too finicky. Alas there was nothing that I could do apart from wait for six long months.

I did get baptised eventually, on the next available date. I was the first sibling in the family to get baptised. People were surprised, because they thought Charlene, being the older would be first. Nevertheless it seemed I was ready to take the plunge before her. I was anxious yet thrilled at the same time. I felt that getting baptised was the right thing to do; I believed that getting baptised would hinder me from giving into temptation as I would now be accountable and wanted to dedicate myself to Jehovah. It was a serious and quiet occasion, as it always is and as I stepped out from behind the curtain all eyes were on me, it was silent and the large auditorium at Bowes Road was full of people watching on. I stepped into the pool full of water I made a silent prayer to God and as I was dipped completely into the water and back out again I felt transformed. I received so much attention that day, something that I loved; everyone congratulating me, giving me cards and hugs, welcoming me into Jehovah's kingdom and wishing me well. It was nice and I felt somewhat lighter, mentally. I was happy to be baptised and I took it seriously and being baptised certainly kept me out of trouble... well just a bit.

Chapter 8

Frivolous Activity

Charlene and I discovered an off license just down the road from where we lived, and somehow we developed the habit of going there for sweets practically every evening. The guys who ran the shop had a lot to do with it. It was run by three Asians brothers who were pretty good looking, a lot older than us. Each time we went there, we all talked and messed about and we hung around for ages, well for as long as we could get away with it without mum knowing. I found the visits to the off license exciting and looked forward to going with great anticipation.

One day Charlene went for a ride in a van with one of them and left me waiting for her. I was not happy because Charlene was gone for ages and I dare not go home without her, so I waited anxiously on my own with the others. When Charlene turned up I let her know that I was not happy with the fact that she had abandoned me like that. Charlene would not tell me what she did in the van.

One day in the off license a young woman walked in wearing tight white jeans, she looked quite sexy and the guys were just in awe of her. I felt so inadequate and wondered how he (the one I fancied) could look at that other woman like that? 'What about me?' I thought we had some special connection. Maybe it was because I was short and fat and no matter what, my legs would never be that long and slender.

On another occasion Charlene and I were off out with mum and we happened to stop in the off license. We tried hard to not let it show that we were very familiar with these guys because we did not want mum to suspect what was going on, although nothing was really going on! I tried to make sure that I didn't make eye contact with my guy, however this proved difficult because by now I got butterflies every time I saw him and fed off of his attention. When we left the shop my mum said "What are you doing? I saw you! You were flirting." Innocently I said "What's flirting?" It was then that I realised what flirting was. All that eye contact and the fluttering of the eyelashes and the secret glances, my mother was very aware what was going on, and even though we tried to disguise it, she could see it all very clearly. Luckily we didn't meet with too much of a reprimand, especially as we did not realise that we were indeed flirting...

There came a time when Charlene and I took one of our usual trips to the off licence for our daily dose of flirting. Only to find our friends were not there. We assumed our guys were taking a break, but after several times of not seeing them we finally plucked up the courage and asked for them and were told that the shop was under new management. I could not believe what I was hearing; I was devastated; that awful feeling came back again. I was very upset and could not cope without my daily fix. Life became dull until one day on my way to school I took a different route and I saw his car in the driveway of a house. I recognised it because it was blue and white and it was the same registration number so I was sure it was his car. I was shocked and ecstatic, I had found where my true love lives. I felt it was god's will that I managed to find him by my taking a different route to school. So after much coercing I asked Lara to knock on the door and ask for him to see if he would be my boyfriend. I missed him so much. I was so very nervous with knots in my stomach waiting around the corner for the answer. When Lara finally finished I was eagerly awaiting the news, she told me what he had conveyed to her; he already had a girlfriend. 'What? He already had a girlfriend? What? How could he do this to me? How dare he?' I thought. I was mortified and that feeling of devastation and heartbreak came back yet again. I dealt with this news in my usual way...

Chapter 9

New York – 1984

Leaving school was great; I could not wait to get out into the big wide world. I did not do brilliantly at school – I managed to get four O'Levels, two CSE's, two RSA's and a Pitman's qualification. My last day was full of excitement, no formal ceremonies just lots of egg and flour thrown about and boys fondling girls. It was all a bit much for me and luckily for me I was not fondled.

The excitement of leaving school was no match for the excitement of my first visit to New York with Charlene. You see our dad had finally managed to send for us to spend our summer in New York. It was all very exciting to say the least. At last, after promises year after year that we would be sent for the time had finally arrived.

My sister and I were novice flight passengers and we did not know what to expect – I was 16 and Charlene was 17 so we were old enough to travel alone, however, we were very nervous and apprehensive. My mother took us to the airport with one of the brothers' from the Kingdom Hall. I could see the fret and worry on my mother's face, we had never flown before and we had not been parted from her for more than a week and here we were preparing for a journey of a lifetime to spend six weeks in the Big Apple with our dad. As we said our goodbyes there were many tears and off we went through customs and onto the plane.

The journey was pretty awful despite the nice cabin crew. As the plane took off we ensured we were strapped in and held on tightly to the arm rests, closing our eyes at the same time. The first hurdle was over, it wasn't too bad and then we eagerly looked forward to the mealtimes. We brought loads of sweets and chocolates for the journey as we heard that plane food was not very pleasant. We munched away on our delights and the plane food, watched the in-flight movies, and argued our way through the flight. Surviving the landing was even more distressing than the take-off, the plane moved from side to side and up and down, it felt rough and there we were again holding on for dear life praying to Jehovah for a safe landing. Due to the anxiety and overindulgence we felt quite nauseous. Charlene was so very scared of the flight, more so than I was. Needless to say, by the end of the journey we were just about ready to throw up all the contents of our stomach. We managed to get through it as best we could and once we had landed excitement gripped us once again knowing that it would not be long before we would see our dad. We had not seen him in eight years or so.

Once we had cleared through passport control and customs we walked through dubiously trying to hide the foul mood that we had towards each other. We saw our dad at a distance and he was accompanied by some old looking woman (which later turned out to be his wife) her young daughter Tasha (who kept calling my dad "daddy") which we resented with a passion, and our dad's friend a youngish looking slender man who drove. It was all hugs and kisses with nervousness attached.

New York was huge, the streets were wide and the cars were just as wide, ugly looking things really. Yellow taxis could be seen everywhere and it was sweltering, you could actually see the heat. Luckily the journey from JFK Airport to my dad's home was only 30 minutes.

When we arrived at the apartment in Cornelius Avenue we got out of the car and entered the hallway. It was a two apartment building and ours was on the first floor. Up the stairs and through the door was a dark narrow corridor and immediately to your right was a door which led to the living room and at the end of the living room there was another door that led to a bedroom which belonged to our older brother Hudson. At the other end of the living room was a door to another bedroom which is where we were to sleep. We had to share with Tasha! The bedroom wasn't much to look at; the closet had curtains instead of doors. There was another door to this bedroom which led directly into my dad's room and as you walked through his room there was another door to the right which led into the kitchen, which was a good size. Along the corridor on the right hand side was the bathroom which had no windows, so was quite dark. I couldn't help thinking what a small place with so many doors. I had this vision that my dad was living in a big mansion with loads of rooms, but that vision was quickly shattered when I was faced with the reality of his small three-bedroom apartment.

The refrigerator was huge, you did not have to bend down to look into it and it was jam packed with loads of food. I thought to myself, this is going to be great! It took a while to feel relaxed and comfortable around these strangers. It was odd meeting Hudson our older brother because we did not even know he existed, but he was nice enough and we developed a good relationship with him. He always looked out for us when we were there; it was reassuring having an older brother. Connie, Sandra, and Dirk all came over at the weekend and once their summer holidays kicked in they stayed over. It reminded me of the time when we all shared the one single bed when we were little. Only this time, Dirk shared with Hudson and we had Tasha tagging along.

New York was absolutely mind blowing – we went on many trips and picnics, visiting The Statue of Liberty, Staten Island, The Twin Towers, and Central Park – in fact we were proper tourists. Our dad even took us to a night club with all his friends, and that was exciting, I had only ever been to one night club before in London and I had to sneak out and lie to my mother in order to do that. At the club one of my Dad's friends called Andrew asked me to dance, it was the first time that I had danced so close to a man before and I was a little nervous. He told my dad that he liked the way I danced so softly. I later developed a crush on Andrew.

My dad seemed to enjoy showing us off to his friends and he could not have given us a better holiday. He took us shopping and spent hundreds on us, new clothes, bags, shoes, purses, jewellery and I felt very special. We ate out a lot which I really enjoyed; the diners were particularly fascinating as we had brunch and ice cream sodas and cheese cakes. We often got Chinese takeaways and KFC which tasted much nicer than the ones in England and the servings in New York were huge. I felt like I had come home.

The weekend started on a Friday evening and there was always some kind of party in someone's basement. It was the highlight of our week. The men folk played dominoes, the kids hung out and the women were there trying to get the attention of the men cooking some kind of soup and selling drinks. Good music was always playing loudly and we would all get together and dance and have fun. This was the first time that I was allowed to drink alcohol without it being rationed and I took to it like a fish to water. I enjoyed drinking Heineken from the bottle and became a dab hand at opening the bottle with my teeth when a bottle opener could not be found. Drinking alcohol made me feel alive!

On Saturday nights it was a different basement and this went on till the early hours of the morning so no little kids were there. It was more grown up and my dad would dress up for this one. This is where we were allowed to have rum and black, it was glorious, very sweet and it certainly went to my head. We often got carried away with drinking but dad did not seem to mind. As long as he was there it did not matter and I expect he was keeping an eye on us! Feeling tipsy was fun!

We also made an effort to attend the meetings at our local Kingdom Hall, particularly on the Sunday and made new friends. My dad was not too keen about this, especially when they invited us around for dinner or picnics. But we felt we should make the effort and do our duties as Jehovah's Witnesses even though we were on holiday. Besides, they were real nice.

New York was fun it was fast moving and exciting and having to come home to dreary old England was not a happy prospect. The last day of our vacation was extremely depressing, with loads of tears. Everyone came to see us off at the airport; it was like one great big family outing. It was painful letting go and going our separate ways, I don't think I remember a time when I cried that much. I wanted to stay and be with my dad and live the life of partying, but alas our tickets were booked and we had to return to our home with our mum and four brothers.

Despite this returning home was still quite exciting, we had missed our brothers and our mum and we had presents for them all. They were all happy to see us back safe and sound. Everything seemed different the refrigerator was tiny as we had to bend down to get food out of it unlike the ones in New York. My brothers even complained about us trying to speak with an American accent; they thought we were putting it on, but the accent had rubbed off on us; we were there for six weeks! It did not take long for normality to set in though.

Whilst in America my father took us to the opticians, I normally wore those brown square national health glasses (you know them ugly looking cheap things). They only came in three colours, brown, pink and blue! I was short sighted at the age of nine and had no choice but to wear them. It ran in my family and when I was diagnosed I was none too pleased about having to wear glasses. Children at school were mean, and would call me 'four eyes, goggle eyes,' etc. So when my dad took us to an American optician and had the money to pay for our glasses I was over the moon. I chose these large round peach and crystal looking frames which suited my round face. Charlene got similar ones, but hers were burgundy, not so 'in your face'. I loved my glasses and was happy to ditch the brown ones. Before long that style of glasses hit the streets in London.

I felt more grown up now, had a new image and felt a little bit more attractive than I had ever felt. I decided to visit my old school to see my friends who had stayed on for the sixth form; Lara was one of them. When I arrived it felt good because I was receiving a lot of attention, everyone wanted to hear about my trip to New York. Here I was, this poor little girl now telling everyone of the fantastic time I had in the Big Apple. I received many compliments too, about how great I looked. For once life seemed good, or was it?

Chapter 10

First Job – 1984 - 1985

I somehow wished I had stayed on to do A levels, but felt I had to follow in my aunts' footsteps and work as a secretary. My aunty Gean spoke to her boss about me looking for work as a trainee and he agreed to meet me. So one day I got on the 25 bus from outside my home to begin my journey into the West End for the first time by myself. I was given the address and directions and felt fairly confident that I would be able to find my way in good time. The journey went on for ages and I slowly became impatient and nervous, but felt comfort in the fact that my aunty would be at the office also.

I came off the bus at what I thought was the right stop, Oxford Circus, and it was not long before I realised that I disembarked at the wrong stop. I was in Holborn instead of Oxford Circus, I started to panic and realised I was too far away to continue my journey on legs. I had two options which I found quite distressing, use the remainder of my money to get home safely or use it to get to Oxford Circus despite not having much faith in myself. If I got on another bus that meant I would have to find my way to the office where my aunty Gean would be able to give me some extra money for my bus fare home. By now my mind was in such a state, I was scared and did not have the courage to ask anyone for assistance. I felt determined and took the risk of getting on another bus towards Oxford Circus, however I managed to pluck up the courage and ask the conductor to let me know when we arrived at Oxford Circus, which he did and I managed to find my way. What a relief! I arrived at the office late and in a bit of a state and rambled on to my aunty about my ordeal and she consoled me enough so I could pull myself together.

I met with her boss Mr Brown, who ran a very small computer training company, he needed a Junior Secretary/Receptionist to run the office when my aunty was not working, she worked there on a part time basis. Peter took me on under the Youth Training Scheme, and because I was employed under this scheme it meant I received £27 per week rather than £15. I had to attend Sight and Sound College on the Charing Cross Road twice a week to study bookkeeping and shorthand as I needed to acquire those skills for the job. I enjoyed the training and achieved a diploma for each of the subjects; bookkeeping at 76% and shorthand at a whopping 92%.

The job was ok, although the days that my aunty did not work and Mr Brown was out of the office training were not so good. I felt extremely lonely and bored especially when I had to put training manuals together – photocopying and manually collating the manuals into individual binders, very mind numbing stuff for such a bright gal. Whilst in the office I would often go off into my own little world. I often chewed gum, and Mr Brown told me not to when in the office because it did not sound right when I answered the phone. I was very upset by this and thought 'How dare he reprimand me in this way, who does he think he is? He is not my dad!' it really cut me and I went into the toilets to cry. Another occasion I arrived at work after my morning at college and he sarcastically said "What time do you call this, working part time now are we?" I immediately wanted to cry, but managed to hold it down and responded by reminding him that I had been to college, he seemed quite embarrassed and was very apologetic. However, the damage was done, he upset me and it did not stop me from going into the toilets and crying my eyes out. I was, it seems, overly sensitive.

Although I enjoyed the independence of working and having my own money, I found this change in life lonely and it was at this time that I developed a severe liking for chocolate, I was eating at least three bars a day, I just had to have them no matter what. It was as if something inside was pulling me to the chocolate and it was beyond my control to stop it. I also spent my lunch hours shopping or eating McDonalds, Wendy Burgers or Pie and Mash on my own.

My second trip to New York came in the summer of 1985 which was very much like the first trip in many aspects. However, our father did not take as much time off work and he did not spend as much money on us. In fact Charlene and I paid for the flights ourselves. We were working now, so we could afford it. Being back in New York felt good for me, I enjoyed being around my dad and my other sisters, it was nice having a younger sister and we became quite close.

One of the local boys in the neighbourhood by the name of Dinx took a shine to me and wanted me to be his girlfriend, he was so keen and very sweet but I did not really fancy him, although I liked the attention. He was well built, quite muscular and his colouring a little lighter than myself. His lips were full and he had small eyes, he was very sweet, so why didn't I fancy him? Secretly I liked an older guy by the name of Junior who kept winking and smiling at me. Dinx was there, eager to please and be my boyfriend and I was not really interested, but instead I was interested in Junior an older guy, slightly darker skinned than myself and good looking, but quite skinny and always wearing a hat, just like my dad did, he hardly spoke to me but kept winking from afar. The more he winked the more my crush on him developed to the point where I felt I loved him. This behaviour continued despite the fact that I was still a Jehovah's Witness; however whilst I was on holiday it didn't seem that important as I was having fun.

By the time the end of our trip arrived, I was not ready to leave so I decided that I would stay a bit longer. I truly felt that I wanted to live in America and considered the idea quite seriously. My sister left as planned and I asked her if she would kindly inform my boss and aunt that I would not be going back to my job. Needless to say, my sister forgot! I received a call from my aunt saying that Mr Brown had hit the roof and thought of me as rude and inconsiderate by not informing him. I explained it all to my aunt and asked her to apologise to him for me, and tell him that my sister was given a message which she forgot to impart and that I did not intentionally refuse to not turn up without a word. I felt really awful because I did not want anyone to think badly of me. I actually hated my sister for not giving that message, I even wondered if she did it on purpose.

The rest of my time in New York was excellent – so it seemed. I ate during the day because everyone was either at work or school. So it was just me and my food, oh and soap operas, General Hospital, All My Children, The Bold and the Beautiful, one after the other. I could not wait for the weekends when my sisters would come over to stay and we would go over the road to the basement party on Friday's, Saturday's a club with our dad and Sunday's another basement party a few blocks away. My sisters and I would get a lot of male attention, but the guys had to be very careful because my dad was rather protective of us. He still allowed us to drink and dance with the guys, but he always had that watchful eye wide open. In fact he would often tell us about which guys liked us and the compliments he would get about his beautiful daughters – we became known as 'Dougie's Daughters'.

One day I found out that Junior was seeing another girl by the name of Opal, Dinx's sister, their father ran the basement parties on Irving Avenue which we would go to on a Friday. When I heard the news I was mortified and felt so betrayed. I had danced with him real close and allowed him to touch my breasts, did that not mean anything? I ran home sobbing my poor heart out. Words could not describe how I felt that day. When I arrived home my older brother Hudson was there and he was very concerned and wanted to know why I was crying. I eventually managed to mutter out the words "Junior was leading me on, and I thought I was his girl". Hudson was not at all sympathetic; he just got a little angry and said that none of those guys are worth crying over. When my dad came home that day he was told about my crying episode and he was even more unsympathetic than Hudson. In fact, he was shouting and telling me off. I neither heard nor understand much about what he was saying. All I knew was that I felt unloved, rejected, uncared for and abandoned. I decided that it was time to go home; I had put on weight and had spent practically three months in New York; enough was enough. I packed my bags and got my dad to book my flight. I could not deal with men and all this blasted heartache. However, I still visited my dad the following year and again two years after that.

Chapter 11

Working Girl – 1985 - 1986

Returning home was somewhat depressing, back to England where everything was smaller, and back to the Kingdom Hall and the dull life that I led. I had no job, so I decided to sign up with an agency and in no time at all I found a job as a secretary working for the Royal Society in Carlton House Terrace near Piccadilly. The building looked like it used to be a grand stately home and it housed some lovely antique furniture especially in the library. The other secretaries were nice enough, but I did not particularly like my boss. He was an old dithery guy who just got on my nerves and I squirmed when he called me into his office to take shorthand. We had a tea lady that came round first thing in the morning, then again at 11.00am and in the afternoon at 3.00pm. I would have black coffee in the morning with biscuits and a lemon tea in the afternoon again with biscuits; I always eagerly waited for the tea lady each day, and could feel a little excitement every time I heard her trolley approaching around the corner.

The only thing that kept me going in that job was Clay the post boy. A nice looking blue eyed boy with scruffy blonde hair, who I took a liking to and he seemed to take a liking to me also. Every time he delivered mail into my office he would stop and talk to me – I was getting a high from each conversation, wondering when he would ask me out. Even though I was not allowed to go out with him because of my religion, but that did not stop me from fantasising about the outcome. At times I needed to go to the post room and the butterflies in my stomach would engulf me. Things seemed to feel rather intense with Clay and I; it came to a point that I could not contain myself anymore with the feelings I had inside. So I plucked up the nerve and approached him about us dating or courting and he just flippantly said that he was a Satan worshiper. I did not know why he said that but I freaked out, he knew I was a Jehovah's Witness. 'Did he do that on purpose? Did he not know what it took for me to ask him out?' From that day on although I still had a soft spot for him what he said managed to diffuse my feelings for him. He ended up going out with another girl that worked there and I hated her for that.

I was bored, fed up with working for such an old annoying man and needed a change. So I decided to leave my job; I signed up with Alfred Marks recruitment agency and started temping for them. I eventually ended up back at the Royal Society for a long stint. My old boss was somewhat upset that I had come back working for someone else and was enquiring if he could have me back. He obviously did not realise that the whole point of me leaving was to get away from him. I much preferred temping, I felt like my own person and somewhat free. I became very close to one of the secretaries, Carla was her name, an Anglo Indian lady who was in her early twenties when I met her, she had two young girls and I could not believe that she was as old as she said she was.

Carla and I did nearly everything together, had lunch, booked the computer in the computer room at the same time, left work together. It was great; we had a good laugh and confided in each other about our problems. Carla had a friend by the name of Chris who used to call her and talk about his problems and she would try and help him out. I met him a couple of times, and I took a fancy to him so I asked Carla to try and get us together, but it never actually happened because it turned out that he had a crush on Carla. I was very upset, I felt that nobody wanted me and it just was not fair. We stayed in touch for many years after and I would often visit her and spend time with her family. I developed many fond memories, but we eventually lost touch.

My contract finally ended there and I temped around the area of Piccadilly working for many different companies, I walked out on some bookings because I did not like the way I was spoken to and some bookings I really enjoyed. Some of the places where I worked wanted to take me on permanently, but I was not interested in settling down in one job. I enjoyed the variety of industries, people, offices and the freedom to not work if I did not want to. Temping had its downside, I was always the new girl who had to learn everything from scratch and I was never around long enough to make friends.

This ultimately meant I was often going to lunch on my own, feeling rather lonely. My lunch hour would be spent either eating hamburgers or pies otherwise I would go clothes shopping. I loved fashion and would buy a new outfit every week, maybe even more. Shoes and accessories were also very important as I liked to match my outfits. One sunny day I was wearing a Leopard print skirt with matching top. I really favoured that outfit and felt confident wearing it. However, on this particular day I was walking past a construction site and, as workmen do, they wolf whistled me, with one of them saying with great emphasis, "Phwoar, look at the size of those." I instantly wanted the ground to swallow me up, I felt ashamed, guilty, and dirty and violated all at the same time. The feeling was so strong that I found the nearest clothes shop, went inside and bought myself a big black baggy shirt and quickly changed into it. I then ate chocolate and cake.

I ended up working for the Head Office of Alfred Marks as an HR administration assistant, I really enjoyed the role, it was meaty and a challenge. Sometimes I was late for work and they made such a big deal out of it, I felt that they had no understanding of my journey from East to West and that trains sometimes were delayed. Eventually before the year was up I was made redundant. I cried a great deal over the loss of that job, I felt they were getting rid of me because I was sometimes late. Back to temping I went.

Chapter 12

Unease at Home – 1987

Life at home was not exactly wonderful, I was working; my sister Charlene had met someone from St Lucia, by the name of Gerald a tall dark and very handsome young man and they finally got married. Her wedding was lovely and she looked beautiful. Her colour theme was yellow and she had seven bridesmaids in total. Of course, I was her chief bridesmaid, and my dress was white with yellow spots. However there was a little problem in that it was a little small for me when we bought it, but I loved it so much and promised myself I would slim down in order to get into it. As the wedding day loomed closer and closer I was not getting any slimmer. I was rather distressed, because I loved the dress and I did not have enough money to buy another one, so at the last minute I commissioned one of our church sisters by the name of Jean to alter the dress. Luckily enough the dress had a lot of material so she was able to take some fabric from the bottom of the dress and make it larger at the sides. I was very pleased with the outcome even though I did look huge in the dress.

So Charlene moved out and it was just me, mum and my brothers. I missed my sister and even though she wound me up taking my clothes without asking and just being the big sister, I loved her and pined for her. Mum also started courting Rick again, that eerie man from my childhood. I was not very pleased about him, I just did not take to him, and so I kept my distance. My brothers also did not like him, in fact they loathed him. Mum ended up marrying him much to our disappointment. Her wedding was a small affair at the local registry office in Stratford. It did not feel like a happy and momentous occasion, but dull and gloomy – you see even the extended family did not like Rick. The reception was at my grandparents' house; they had the room and as it was such a small affair there was no need to hire a hall. It was probably the most boring wedding I had ever and would ever attend!

Having Rick in the house was awful. He had this air of self importance, and an expressionless face. He was a tall man, over six foot, slender with a chiselled jaw and dark hair, my mum thought he was handsome, but to me he just looked like a cold, uncaring person, who hardly ever smiled. Apparently he had a back problem, so before long he was not working but claiming disability allowance. My mother was also not working – she never did go out to work much from as far back as I can remember. My youngest brother Troy was still only 13 when she married Rick.

When Rick joined the family our housekeeping money that we paid to our mother went up. Jay and I resented this very much as we felt that it only went up to pay for the lazy man that our mother decided to marry. This was wrong but my mother was being controlled by this bastard. I tended to keep myself to myself and spent most of my time in my bedroom, listening to music and eating chocolates, sweets and cakes.

When Rick moved in I had to move back into the cold bedroom, the same room that David made Shane, Alvin and myself use when we first moved into the house in 1976 because we were the ones that wet the bed. This time round however, I loved being in it because before I moved into it, we cleared it out and decorated it. We used thick wallpaper on the outside walls to help keep the room warm. It was actually meant for a bathroom, but it was pretty wallpaper with light blue and lilac flowers. The other two walls were papered with woodchip and painted light pink. I purchased a blue/grey carpet, and bought myself a lovely big white wardrobe, matching dressing table and stool with a pink cushion and a bookcase where I placed my music system. It was so cosy now, it became my haven. Even my curtains were beautiful – venetian blinds – they were flowery and frilly matching my room colours.

We were all still active in our religion and my brothers and I would often journey out after my mum and Rick, apart from the times he stayed at home due to his so-called painful back. Even when he did go, we preferred to walk than to go with them in his car. I had started learning to drive by now and failed my test four times, on each occasion my nerves always got the better of me. Every time I was told that I failed I could not help but cry in the car on the journey home, I always believed that the examiner was being unfair. I would snatch the piece of paper out of my instructors' hands and would secretly blame them for not doing their job properly. I would get home, slam the car door and the front door, run up to my room, cry or go get some chocolate or biscuits. I felt so rubbish and that nothing ever went right for me. My younger brother even passed before I did, why was life so damn unfair?

I was determined so I purchased my first car in order to get more practice, it was mustard Austin Allegro with a brown roof and I loved my new car. When I got it home, I cleaned it out from top to bottom, inside and out. I eventually passed my test on my fifth try and was over the moon. I was independent!

My sister would spend loads of time back at our house, even though she was married. It was good to have her around. We were both struggling with our weight and were always looking for quick fixes. We found this so called Dr in Ilford who supplied people with slimming tablets and tablets to remove excess water. We were so happy that someone told us about him. So every Monday evening we would trek down to Ilford with our grandmother in tow to get our tablets. Initially he came across very professional and gave us a consultation, weighed us and gave us a diet sheet. Eventually it became routine; he just weighed us, noted it down and took the money in exchange for the tablets which were contained in tiny brown envelopes. No appointments were necessary; we would just turn up at his house, where he turned his conservatory into a surgery with a large waiting area. We would get so impatient if we turned up and saw loads of people waiting. We just wanted our tablets and wanted them quickly.

The tablets were like tiny little miracles, they stopped that hunger feeling altogether. In fact, once I had breakfast I did not feel like eating for the rest of the day, it was amazing; and the weight just fell off. However, the tablets often made my heart beat too fast and gave me a very dry mouth and what with the rumours that the Dr's activities were illegal we decided to give them up only to return to them at times when we became desperate once again to lose weight for a certain occasion.

Chapter 13

First True Love

I remember the day I saw him we were at the meeting on a Sunday morning and there he was. In my eyes he was just so handsome, this young fresh looking man – he was a nice chocolate tone not quite dark chocolate but a little darker than milk chocolate, his lips were perfectly shaped and they looked as if he were purposely pouting his lips. He had a gap tooth just like me. After the meeting I told my sister, mother, Melissa and Michelle – we always walked to and from the meetings with them and their mother Ruth. I told them "That is the man I am going to marry." Everyone was shocked at what I said; they told me I cannot say that, I couldn't be so sure. But I knew he would be mine, you see, he reminded me of my dad – his deep eyes and his colouring were just like my dads'.

Each time I went to the meetings I was filled with excitement about the prospect of seeing him. His name was Anthony and he was new to the country, he came from Sierra Leone, I had never heard of it before, he was not baptised but had walked into the Kingdom Hall asking for a study. He had spoken to the witnesses back in Sierra Leone and was now in England studying Marketing. I would always make sure that I was in eye shot of him so that he would notice me, but it did not seem to work. So I had to make it happen. He was even attending the same book study as me on Whytville Road (these book studies were held at people's homes on a Tuesday or

Thursday night) which meant there was no chance he could miss seeing me. All I could ever manage was a smile if that; I became such a heap of slush whenever I saw him.

Time for action! I told my brother in law Gerald to let him know that someone liked him and to give him certain clues. I did not want to make it completely obvious and easy for him. However I think the clues he was given were probably quite evident. But I did not care; I wanted him especially before all the other hungry church sisters got their hands on him.

One Saturday Charlene and I were off out with mum and they were keeping me waiting, I was becoming so impatient and was walking off from them in an attempt to hurry them up. Some strange guy was trying to get my attention which angered me even more than having to wait for them. I gave him a very dirty look which hopefully put him in his place. You see, I got that all the time, men always whistling and trying to talk to me, I always found it very offensive, and it made me so angry; I thought of them as perverts. Mum and Charlene finally caught up with me and we carried on our way, walked to the 101 bus stop and got on the bus at Manor Park Broadway. Charlene and I sat upstairs while mum stayed downstairs. When we got to the top of the bus guess who was sitting up there? Yes there he was looking all suave and shy the love of my life. As I said hello to him I became all limp. He mentioned that he was trying to call me earlier to say that my sister was calling me down the road. I was so embarrassed I did not know where to put my face – he was the guy that I gave the dirty look; I was surprised he was still alive as my looks could really kill! I apologised profusely not wanting him to think I was as awful as my dirty looks. How could I not recognise the man of my dreams – my eyesight had failed me! He got off the bus pretty much straight away; probably because he could not handle the tension. I was a bit put out about it, but was happy that we at least made some contact.

After one of the book study meetings Anthony and I got talking. He shyly asked me if I was the girl that Gerald was talking about. I was rather embarrassed that he knew; 'Did I make it that obvious?' I wondered. Anthony was chuffed and said he liked me also. I couldn't help but grin from ear to ear, I was over the moon, he liked me too; this was just brilliant at last someone I liked also liked me for a bleeding change. We would meet up after meetings and spoke for hours on the phone. He would visit me at my home on Sunday's after the morning meeting.

It was on one of those Sundays that he just got hold of me and pressed his body against mine. I was startled not knowing what to do and before I could take my next breath he kissed me gently on my lips; I responded instinctively as it was my first ever kiss, I felt as if I was floating. Up went one leg backwards as I leant into him feeling his strong embrace; just like they do in the movies. That kiss sealed our relationship as a couple, he was my first proper boyfriend and I was extremely happy, the happiest I had been in a very long time. I wanted to spend every waking moment with Anthony; I really felt a connection with him and I knew he felt it too.

On one occasion when we arranged to meet up in Woodgrange Road, I was excited at the prospect of seeing him. He was carrying a heavy bag with his college books and asked me to carry it for him. I was a little, no, a lot, shocked and thought I don't know how it is in your country but in this country the men carry the bags not the women. I did not carry the bag for him but did not have the guts to tell him what I really thought about that request, I just shyly refused. We went back to his place in Fowler Road; he lived there with his sister Olga, and his uncle Samuel.

It was a medium sized maisonette with three bedrooms; he had the smallest bedroom which only had space for a single bed and a small wardrobe. We spent our time listening to music, talking and petting. There were times when he would want to go a little further but I was far too scared and would stop him in his tracks. I felt a little bad going back to his place after that although it did not stop me. You see, as Christians we were supposed to be chaperoned and not allowed to be in a house by ourselves. However coming back to my place all the time meant we did not have enough quality time on our own as my house was always full of people.

Anthony worked for Casey Jones burger bar in Charing Cross at the time and I would often go and visit him there – free food free food. I sometimes turned up there without telling him in advance, I liked to surprise him. I would wake up early and go and see him before I went to work or I would go during my lunch break. He always seemed so pleased to see me, we would talk for a bit, have a little kiss and then off I went to work feeling warm inside and ready for the world.

My family liked Anthony, he was always welcome at my home and my brothers treated him a bit like their own brother. Rick, however, was too nosey and would often take the chaperoning business beyond the call of duty. I wish he would just mind his own bleeding business and go rest his back! Anthony was quite a secretive person and did not really want the people in the Kingdom Hall to know that we were seeing each other whereas I did. I wanted people to see us as a solid item, I thought it important that we sit together at the meetings, but he was not having it. I started putting pressure on him and he finally succumbed only to find that the elders were very concerned with our union.

They wanted to speak to us privately; we were called into the room upstairs of the Kingdom Hall, as I walked slowly up the stairs trepidation consumed me. We entered the room to be greeted by three of the congregation elders all seated looking at us with a somewhat contemptuous look on their faces. They looked business like in their dull grey suits; in fact one of them looked as if he had eaten too many pork pies the night before, with his stomach hanging over his belt! We were prompted to take a seat opposite them and they proceeded to ask what was going on between us. We informed them that we were courting to which they responded that in no uncertain terms could the courtship continue; it had to end immediately because Anthony was not yet a baptised brother and I was simply getting in the way of his progress. I was mortified, how dare they dictate what we should and should not do I thought. Despite my anger we agreed to their demands although I knew deep down that we would continue seeing each other because we loved each other so much.

Thus began our secret meetings, it was exciting. I would go to his house so no one would know. I would tell my mum that I was going to see my friend Lara, who by now was studying with me to become a Jehovah's Witness and as I lived around the corner it worked out well for me. In fact, I would often see her first and then drop by Anthony's. It felt good that I could now tell her all about my boyfriend. Things started to hot up between Anthony and myself and we were now doing heavy petting. I was still a little apprehensive especially when he wanted to do certain things. Certain things I was totally against. Because of this Anthony told me, "I would be very boring." Those words hurt me very much and caused mix feelings of hating him for saying that and feeling pressured into pleasing him lest I should lose him. I did not want to commit fornication, it was a sin in the eyes of Jehovah to have sex before marriage and I wasn't about to do that. So in my eyes it was best to play it safe to stop the temptation from going that far.

One day I was at his house as usual chilling out upstairs. His buzzer went off and we both froze and wondered who was at the door. Anthony went to answer the buzzer and informed me that it was Harry, the brother who conducted Anthony's personal bible studies. 'Oh shit!' I thought, my heart starting to beat faster. 'What was I going to do?' He was on his way up to the flat by now and I could not escape even if I wanted to. So Anthony suggested I just wait upstairs until he finished his bible study. I was annoyed because how could he have forgotten that he was meant to be having his bible study anyway. That hour of waiting and trying hard not to move around too much in case Harry could hear me was the longest hour of my life thus far. I was scared and there was nothing I could do but just sit still until Harry went home. I was very relieved when he left although once he departed Anthony felt guilty after his studies about having me there and said it was best if I went home which did not please me one little bit.

Casey Jones often laid on staff parties, which Anthony invited me to come along to with him. One of those parties was held in the West End, we journeyed there together by tube. Anthony's colleagues were present, most of them he knew well, and he introduced me to a handful of them. I felt a little out of place because it was not a Christian gathering, however we spent time together talking and dancing and just enjoying each other's company. At some point Anthony said, "Wait there, I won't be very long," I said, "OK" and off he went. I felt weird sitting there on my own, believing that everyone was watching me. I could be very paranoid and fearful at times – especially in alien surroundings. I also found it difficult to make conversation with people I was not familiar with. At least twenty minutes went by and Anthony had not returned. I started to panic felt fearful and alone for some strange reason. I mustered up the courage to go and look for him only to find him dancing with a girl. I was deeply upset and livid so decided to walk back to our spot, put on my lovely, long, warm fur collar coat which I had not long bought, and walk out of the venue with my head held high. Anthony followed closely behind begging me not to be so dramatic and apologising. I was not interested in what he had to say, I was far too upset and humiliated and trying not to show it.

By the time I reached outside I was shouting at him and crying. "How could you do that to me and you know I don't know anyone there?," and "Who is she anyway? I am supposed to be your girlfriend." He just kept trying to appease me and told me to wait whilst he went to get his coat. I carried on walking and he finally caught up with me and we went home. I told him that he should never do that to me again, as it was just not on and he agreed and was very sorry. So I forgave him, until next time...

James was one of Anthony's best friends from Sierra Leone and he came over to Anthony's to meet me. He seemed pleasant enough but later Anthony told me that James was very surprised that he went out with me. I asked "Why?" to which he responded "Well James said that you were the fattest girl I have been out with and he did not realise that I liked fat girls." I was deeply offended by those words. How very dare he call me fat? I was not that fat anyway, at least I had a pretty face, which Anthony assured me of. What a horrible thing to say, I just resigned to the fact that James was jealous of Anthony!

Meeting Anthony's sister Olga and her boyfriend Femi was just as bad. His sister was in my eyes the most difficult person I had ever met. It seemed as if she took an instant disliking to me. I found her very unpleasant and miserable. As time went on however, our relationship got better, she saw how much I loved her brother and began to accept me. The four of us were at a party which was thrown by one of their friends. It was a nice enough party and we were having a good time, until Anthony disappeared. The rest of us were practically ready to leave so we went looking for him. We found him in the hallway talking to some floozy – they were being very intimate in their manner and continued to talk in that fashion even when I turned up to let him know that we were ready to go. Once again I was outraged; 'Was he really doing this to me again?' I felt so insignificant. I went off on one and started calling the girl some awful names in one of my rages whilst Olga was trying to calm me down, albeit she agreed with what I was saying. I could not understand why he would treat me that way. Needless to say he apologised and I forgave him – again.

Despite this behaviour Anthony was progressing in the religion and decided that he wanted to get baptised. I was pleased for him as I was already baptised and it meant we could progress as a couple. However, he wanted us to take a break in order for him to concentrate on his up and coming baptism and focus on his special baptism questions over the coming months. The only words that I heard were 'break up,' I believed he was no longer interested in me, and the thought of not seeing him would destroy me. I had no choice but to agree with him, after all we were not even meant to be seeing each other as it was. I was falling apart inside but outwardly held it together, I felt desperately lonely and scared and I just did not know how to handle this.

That evening I arrived home and did not show how upset I was, after all, how could I when everyone assumed we were not seeing each other anyway. I did not know what to do or who to turn to. I could not envisage living without Anthony for any length of time. That empty feeling engulfed me in such a way that I had never felt before. I became numb and shut myself down. I was on medication (amitriptyline) for migraines. A thought came to my mind and before I could get rid of that thought, in sheer desperation I went and got some water from the kitchen and walked back to my bedroom and slowly started popping the pills – I was taking an overdose (as I type these words, my fingers can hardly move). I don't know how many I took; 9 maybe 10 but as I took them, my mind went blank as nothing really mattered anymore. I then fell asleep; hoping never to awaken again.

The following morning I woke up, completely oblivious about what I had done the night before. However as I walked to the bathroom to get ready for work my muscles would not work, they felt like jelly and I collapsed half way, I was frightened and it was then that I remembered what I had done, I was reminded of the events leading up to the time I took the overdose and felt extremely annoyed to say the least that it had not worked. My body started to shake and I became fearful so I mustered up some energy and called my brother Jay, who was awake getting ready for work. I told him to get mum; he was asking what was wrong. He called out to my mother who woke up and came running worried out of her head. They managed to get me back into my bed and started questioning me if I felt ill. I could not speak, I could not look them in the eye, and I did not even want to be there. All I was able to do was show them the bottle of empty pills.

They were panicking by now and the rest of the house was rising. They called the Doctor who came round as soon as possible. I vaguely remember him checking me over and advising them to give me lots of fluid to flush out the tablets and reassuring them that I would be ok. 'What a shame,' I thought. Throughout the day family members came to visit to see how I was. I heard comments like "This is a cry for help." "Why did she do it?" And "Does Anthony know?" – I just dosed in and out of sleep resenting the fact that it did not work and that I had to keep going to the toilet due to the amount of fluid I had to drink.

Anthony came to see me, but he did not seem to be that concerned that I had done this because I needed so much to be with him, he looked like he resented me for doing it. Looking back now, who could blame him? I don't remember much after that until the time came when Anthony got baptised. That's all I lived for, the day when he would get baptised and we could be together once again.

Chapter 14

Engagement - 1988

Not long after Anthony got baptised I put the pressure on him for us to start seeing each other, however, this was done in secret. Anthony did not want others to know that we got back together so quickly. I started to feel like a dirty little secret once again, however I conceded even though I did not see a problem with it myself, 'He is baptised now what's their problem?' I thought. Their stance was that he needed time to mature spiritually before getting involved. 'Bollocks!' I thought to that. I did not like all the secrecy, I wanted us to be out in the open – how nice it would be for us to walk into the Kingdom Hall together as a couple. Alas, it was not to be for now, so I just put up with the situation for a while. However, before long I was at it again, putting the pressure on to become public. After all, we weren't really doing anything wrong.

One Saturday Anthony wanted to take me shopping, but he would not say what for. He said it was a surprise and immediately I thought, 'We must be going to get an engagement ring, how exciting.' So we set off in my little Austin Allegro down to Stratford. I was bursting with excitement at this prospect, and sat in the passengers' seat for fear the excitement would get in the way of my driving us safely down to Stratford. We went straight to Argos, which I thought was a little odd, but then remembered that they did have a jewellery section in there. However, that was not where he was heading at all; he was looking in the catalogue, 'OK,' I thought, 'Maybe he needs to see what the ring looks like in the catalogue first.' However, he skipped that section and started looking in the section for car stereos. I was furious, mortified, and upset all at the same time but dare not show it. He was buying a stereo for my car and he looked so pleased with himself. 'How very fucking (well maybe not 'fucking,' being I was a good Christian gal)... sweet of him,' I thought with a fake smile on my face, I found it difficult not to show my disappointment.

As time progressed Anthony finally agreed that we should go public with our courtship. It made me somewhat happier, because at least we could sit together as a proper courting couple at the meetings. Things between us were good; we spent a lot of time together enjoying each other's company. Anthony was often round my house he was always welcome in our home the same as before. There came a point when mum wondered when we were going to get engaged, 'Thank you!' I thought; relieved that I was not the only one that was wondering!

The only problem with Anthony visiting was the house was always full of people and we did not get much privacy. Rick would always make sure that Anthony did not leave to go home too late and I often wished he would mind his own damn business. On a couple of occasions I managed to sneak him into my room without anyone knowing. It was a challenging task because my room was right at the back of the house upstairs and the staircase of the old Victorian house was quite squeaky. Jay and Alvin had heard him sneak out once, their bedroom was now downstairs right underneath the staircase, and they informed mum and Rick. Needless to say, we were reprimanded for this. 'Nosey little sods,' I thought they would be on my side.

Jay and Rick did not get on at all. One day they had a terrible argument over housekeeping and it led to a fight. I was not present, however, when I returned home Jay had been thrown out of the family home. I was outraged, it was so unfair; he was only 18. That man had a lot to answer for.

Some time had passed; mum and Rick were having an argument. It all blew up and the house was in uproar. I had snuck Anthony in again, so I told him to hide in my wardrobe whilst I went to check things out. It was a bit of a task getting him in there as I had so many clothes and shoes. Mum was sobbing whilst Shane and Troy were arguing with Rick by now, telling him not to put his hands on our mother. She was denying that he had done anything, but her mouth was swollen and she was crying. I was somewhat confused, because here she was injured but denying that he had done anything. Eventually a fight ensued between Rick who was well over six foot tall and Shane who was only about 5'7". It was an awful scene to watch, I started shouting and just wanted to protect my brother, so I quickly ran upstairs to get Anthony down from my room, and because of all the commotion no-one really took much note that he was up in my room. I could not believe that this guy who claimed to have a bad back could fight like he did. I hated him for his lies and for what he was doing to my mum, but she would just stick up for him. I could not wait to get out of that house, and I swore to myself that I would never let a man hit me and treat me like that and get away with it. Some Christian he was!

One Saturday Anthony was acting quite shady and wanted to take me shopping. I was not about to make the same mistake again so I demanded to know what for and he told me straight that it was to get an engagement ring. Even though he had not asked me to marry him exhilaration engulfed me, 'At last, we're getting engaged,' I thought. What a lovely day this was going to be. We chose the ring together it was a pretty little ring – it had cubic zirconium stones around the outside with four larger blue onyx stones in the middle, the whole ring was in the shape of a diamond, although there were actually no diamonds in the ring! It cost a grand total of... wait for it... £40. I was a tad upset that it was so cheap, however, was still very grateful that I was now engaged to the man of my dreams and it was public for all to see.

In all my excitement I just assumed I would wear the ring immediately before leaving the shop. However, Anthony made them box up the ring and he took it and put it safely in his pocket. He dropped me home and said he would see me later; as we were due to go out to a Christian get together. The rest of the day went slowly by as far as I was concerned; my impatience just got the better of me. Later that day as I was getting ready for our evening out with friends Anthony turned up early to pick me up. I was not aware of his arrival until he knocked on my bedroom door. I was practically ready and he approached me, took the ring out of its box and placed it onto its new home, my finger, at the same time saying "You can wear this now." That was it – that was my proposal – 'You can wear this now.' What a crap proposal; in fact it was not even a proposal. But good old Yvonne as I always do just took it with gratitude.

Then off we went to our friends' home for the get together. It was nice to be there, some of our favourite friends were there including Ronnie and Linda a lovely black couple who had two little children a girl and a boy. A perfect little family I thought and I wanted to be just like them. It was not long before people noticed my engagement ring and everyone was so happy for us and congratulated us saying how lovely the ring was. Deep down I was saying to myself that they are just saying it was nice; it was obvious there were no diamonds present, so how could it be lovely. I needed convincing that it was a nice ring and surely enough they were able to convince me because they all seemed genuine enough.

Chapter 15

Wedding Number One - 1989

Time was ticking away; Anthony and I were getting along just fine. We set our wedding date for September 2nd 1989. We had a few months to plan it and invitations were sent out 8 weeks before the wedding. My grandmother (my dad's mum), who happens to share the same birth date as myself, decided that eight weeks was not enough notice and would not be able to attend because there was not enough time for her to find her outfit. This caused a big argument between us. She claimed I gave her the invitation late on purpose because I did not want her to come to my wedding. 'What a feeble excuse,' I thought. Eight weeks was more than enough time, no-one else was complaining. She is one of those typical old fashioned Jamaicans who were not keen on our brothers from the African continent. 'Stuff her,' was my reaction to that. I did not care anyway.

Wedding plans were well under way; my dress was made by our good family friend Olive. I showed her a picture of the dress I wanted and she copied it for me. It was not exact, because I wanted it slightly different, so that it would be unique. The dress was made from white satin; the bodice was a bustier style which was roughed up with pearl beads sewn in throughout it. The bottom part of the dress was long and full with lace sewn around parts of the bottom half as well as the train which was quite long. I brought myself a beaded tiara, veil and long white gloves as my accessories. The wedding cake was baked by none other than my favourite grandmother. She did a fantastic job. However her icing skills were not professional so we managed to get my brother-in-law Gerald's step mum to ice the cake for us. She charged us £90 to ice a three tier cake which we thought was a good price. However, on the day of delivery she wanted an extra £30 which brought about bad feelings. I reluctantly paid for it because I felt I had no choice and it wasn't even that fabulous.

My sister Charlene was a bit annoyed that I had chosen that date to get married as she was eight months pregnant with her first child and could not be bridesmaid. I guess it was a little selfish of me but hey, I had waited too long for this wedding. I had three bridesmaids, my best friend from school, Lara, who by now was a baptised sister; otherwise she could not be one. My aunty Gean and a little girl called Sarah, our good friends' daughter. They wore lilac satin dresses made by – you guessed it – my grandmother. She also made a lot of the food for the reception with some of the sisters helping out by making a dish or two. My granddad had a white BMW and he was my chauffeur. My brother Jay was into photography and he said he would take the pictures for us. It was great that everyone was willing to help us – we had invited 150 guests and the cost of the wedding was minimal because of everyone's kindness.

My dad came over from New York to give me away and he also paid for the alcohol for the wedding. He came with my brother Hudson and youngest sister Sandra. It was lovely to see them and I was very proud and happy that my dad had come to give me away. It was also nice seeing him and my mother in the same room; oh how I wished that they would get together. It was clear they were still attracted to each other, but my mum was being good, being a Christian and all, oh and being married to that man!

The day before the wedding was hectic; I picked up my dress from Olive bringing the money with me for payment. I tried on the dress one last time and it was too big. I had previously asked her to take it in a bit, but I had trouble losing weight for my wedding, because I just found it hard to stick to a diet. However, it seemed like the stress of everything caused me to lose about half a stone, I was quite pleased about that – losing weight without having to try. On the flip side, however, the dress was obviously too big, the bodice was meant to be a tight fit. I reluctantly gave her the money, yet again upset that she had not taken the dress in and it was now too late.

Anthony had come to see me in the evening and we spent some quiet time together in my room. Everyone was busy downstairs. We had a kiss and a cuddle and before long he was getting far too excited and wanted to take it all the way. I put up a resistance as he mumbled, "We are getting married tomorrow, so it doesn't matter." Admittedly it felt good, but at the same time, I felt guilty. I wanted to wait until we were married so everything would be perfect. I insisted that we wait, however, he continued and I felt a little paralysed not sure what to do, before long before I could say 'Boo,' he popped my fucking cherry! In all his excitement it was over before you could say 'Boo hoo,' and I was a little confused about what had just happened. He left pretty swiftly and I just tried to pretend that it did not happen.

My sister Sandra stayed with me the night before the wedding. She provided me with a lot of moral support. We had a bit of a midnight feast in my room, only it wasn't midnight! I did not sleep well that night. My mind was ticking away worrying about the day ahead and excited at the same time. I woke up around 7.00 am no longer able to relax. My mum made a big breakfast which I ate willingly. The phone would not stop ringing and people were constantly popping in. It was frenzied but lovely; all this attention was just great.

My sister Sandra helped me get ready; I did my makeup and hair myself, nothing special, but I was happy enough with how I looked. I stepped into my dress with Sandra's help; I walked slowly towards the mirror in anticipation of what or who would be staring back at me. I was pleasantly surprised to see someone resembling a beauty dressed in white. 'Was that really me?' I thought. I looked great considering I had not spent much money. I could not look at myself for any length of time so quickly turned away from the mirror and leisurely descended downstairs ready for the day. My family were full of compliments.

About an hour or so before the wedding I realised that the flowers I had ordered from the florist had not arrived. I panicked and called the florist. The woman had the dates wrong; even though she had the 2nd in her calendar she somehow assumed that it was the following week. She could not believe her stupidity and nor could I. She apologised profusely and said she would put something together very quickly and rush them over. Well she did and what she brought over was not impressive at all. She could not stop apologising and told me how lovely I looked and gave me back £50 as good measure. 'Too bloody right,' I thought. I was deeply annoyed because my bouquet was not how it should have been. I had chosen to have silk flowers because I wanted to keep the bouquet as a memento; it was meant to be a long, full bouquet instead it was long and thin, but it had to do. The bridesmaid's bouquets were ok, but their hair slides were unsatisfactory and Sarah's one kept falling out of her hair.

My brother was late to take the 'before' photos. I was not impressed; I could not help but think that everything was going to go wrong and that people were deliberately trying to sabotage my big day. When he finally arrived we only had time to take a couple of photographs. I was very pleased with my mum's outfit; she looked very trendy for a change. My dad, the cool dude, looked his usual chic self in his cream suit, his hat and sunglasses.

Here I was a 21 year old young lady walking out of my home for the last time as a single woman; I felt ecstatic. Passersby were stopping to look at the wedding party and it was such a lovely sunny day. My brother took a couple more photographs outside and I made my way to the car which was parked on the main road; my granddad had even put a white ribbon on the car! We drove to Ilford Kingdom Hall which was situated in Kensington Gardens. There was a lot of traffic as is usual on the Romford Road on a Saturday afternoon. We were a little late, but it's a brides' prerogative.

My dad walked me down the aisle and it was a blissful feeling. The aisle of the Kingdom Hall was not long enough for my liking because this hall was short and wide. Our Kingdom Hall in Green Street was not registered for marriages as its length would have been ideal. I was quite nervous once I arrived in front of the alter with my groom waiting for me. We were instructed to sing a hymn or kingdom melody as the

Witnesses called them. Then we sat down and listened to the sermon for about 20 minutes which was given by Ronnie our favourite elder whom we had chosen to marry us. His sermon was lovely; he talked about how important it is to love one another and how man and wife must become one flesh etc etc.

Then it was time for the vows and when he asked if anyone knew of any lawful impediment why we should not marry; I became terribly anxious. My mind went overtime and thought that someone in the audience would stand up and say yes, that they loved him and he loved them too or that we were seeing each other before he was baptised, or that we had done the deed the night before. Thankfully that did not happen. Poor Anthony was so nervous, when he had to repeat his vows, he had a stutter and it became more apparent because of his nerves. I almost wanted to say his words for him. I, however, had no problems; although I was nervous I managed to say my vows quite eloquently with confidence. It all went quite smoothly and when it was time for us to exchange rings, he struggled to put the ring on my finger, it was slightly tight. I did not want to get the next size up in the hope that I would lose enough weight before the wedding. We were pronounced man and wife and I was over the moon; Anthony was invited to 'kiss the bride' and I gladly and willingly pouted my lips in order for him to kiss me. At last I was now his wife.

I was eager to go outside and take more photos as husband and wife, nearly forgetting that we had to sign the register. When the formalities were over, I was lapping up all the attention and took pleasure in everyone coming over to congratulate me. We took photographs outside the hall with family and friends. We then invited all who wanted to join us at

Valentines Park to take more photographs. My husband and I were driven together now in my granddads car. It was lovely being alone in the car with my new husband. We arrived at the park and looked for a picturesque spot to take more photographs and found a lovely spot right next to a pond where swans were swimming. We waited for my brother Jay to turn up with the camera and wondered why he was so late. He finally turned up with his fiancé Gerry with McDonalds. Apparently they were hungry and needed to get some food first. I was none too pleased and made sure he knew, however, he did not seem to care. He took many pictures and to his credit, they were excellent.

We then made our way to the reception which was at a little youth club in East Ham, it was all we could afford as it only cost us £200 to hire. We decorated it with white and lilac balloons, ribbons and flowers. It was nice to see it fully decorated, with all the food and the wedding cake in place. I had expected to be greeted with some music playing in the background as that was the plan. However, to our dismay there was no music system in place. Jay had organised this with one of his friends but his friend had let him down. I was livid. How could we have a wedding without music? I started to feel like the rest of the day was going to be a disaster. Luckily enough, Patrick, one of Anthony's best friends rushed off in order to see what he could do. An hour or so later he was back with a music system in place. Thank God for Patrick.

As the wedding day progressed I could not believe how quickly time was flying by. We ate our meal, which was delicious, I might add. Speeches were made and they were so sentimental. I insisted on giving a speech myself as I liked the public attention. It was also nice hearing my husband say, "...on behalf of my wife and I, we would like to thank you all..." Yes I was a wife at last, and not just any old wife, I was the wife to the man of my dreams. Our first dance was very romantic, it was a special moment.

By the end of the day, people were helping to clear up and we were told to go off and enjoy ourselves. However, I wanted to make sure that everything was cleared up properly and that they knew where things needed to go. But everyone insisted that things would be fine and we were to leave. So off we went back to Anthony's place. Our wedding night was spent at his place, which was now my new home. I was absolutely shattered and was a bit apprehensive about what happens next. To be honest, I just wanted to go to sleep. Except my husband had other plans, he wanted to consummate the marriage; I felt I should oblige. There was no romance, I was nervous and really could not be bothered. I wanted to at least have a shower and put on some sexy nightwear, but it did not turn out like that. I allowed him to do what he had to do without much participation from myself. It did not meet up to my expectations at all. What was all the fuss about? Once it ended I just rolled over and went to sleep.

Unfortunately, we could not afford to go on a honeymoon. Nevertheless, we had planned to go out on day trips in and around London which I enjoyed because I was happy and in love. We even showed up at the Kingdom Hall on the Tuesday for the meeting – everyone was surprised to see us and we were told to go home and enjoy ourselves.

Chapter 16

Married Life

I moved into Anthony's place in Fowler Road, he had the second largest bedroom now. His sister and uncle had both moved on and his mother and cousin were now living there, occupying the other two bedrooms. It was not ideal because I wanted us to live alone with no-one else around. His cousin kept herself to herself really although his mother would cook for us which initially was a welcome treat. She taught me how to cook many traditional West African dishes such as okra stew, fufu, groundnut stew and jollof rice to name a few. It took a while for my dishes to turn out well and I felt resentful that Anthony preferred his mum to cook.

Things were going quite smoothly and on one Sunday two weeks after the wedding Anthony went out in the afternoon, he simply said, "I am going out and I won't be long". I did not question him and off he went. I was all alone in the house and it seemed that he was gone for a very long time. I pottered about making myself busy until all of a sudden a feeling came over me, a feeling that I could not explain, nor could I handle. Without thinking I took myself into the kitchen and got a bottle of wine which was left over from the wedding and started to consume it. Two thirds of a bottle later I passed out on the sofa. I was later awakened by Anthony who had arrived home asking me what I was playing at, holding the bottle in his hand. I was still out of it and I simply said, "I don't know." When I sobered up I myself was perplexed at this somewhat odd behaviour.

Our sex life was also very odd. Each time we made love I would turn my back on Anthony and go to sleep. I did not enjoy it as much as I thought I would especially when I remembered all the heavy petting we engaged in before we married. Eventually I stopped giving him my back after lovemaking, and I started to feel more comfortable with him and would cuddle up and place my head on his manly chest. It was at that point that he finally said, "Now I feel like we are really married."

To enhance our sex life Anthony introduced me to pornography. I was quite shocked and horrified at this for two reasons, one because as Christians we should have not been doing this and two I was just shocked at what the videos contained. The women were being treated in such a degrading way and I found it hard to voice that I did not feel it was right that we watch it. I even hated the fact that there were a couple of times that I would watch it on my own when no-one was around. It made me feel dirty and disgusting. Finally, I found the courage to say that I felt we should not be watching the porn anymore as it just felt so wrong. Anthony agreed and got rid of the videos, so I thought...!

I was not very happy in our home, I so wanted us to have a place of our own, Anthony was more than comfortable where we were; besides he felt we could not afford a home of our own. Alvin and his wife who married not long after us had by now bought a place of their own, it was a lovely little house purchased on a shared ownership basis. The house was newly built and it looked perfect. I wanted one of our own. I spoke to

Anthony and managed to convince him to at least consider the idea of buying a place of our own.

He eventually warmed to the idea and we got in touch with the Housing Association and started the process. The second property we viewed was in Beckton, Partridge Close. It was a lovely Close with shrubs and trees and most of the houses were semi-detached with their own driveways. Number 16 was tucked away in a corner with number 15. As I entered the front door I was taken aback, I instantly felt at home, this was the house for us I thought.

As I walked into the house there was a winding wooden staircase with black metal rails. It was definitely a stunning feature of the house and I loved it. The fully fitted kitchen was opposite, it was small and compact with a window looking out towards the front garden which housed shrubs and rose bushes. There was not much of a hallway as the living room led straight on from it. It was a fair size and the window also looked onto the front garden, it was a large window so the room was very bright and airy.

Up the winding stairs on the top of the landing was an airing cupboard large enough to put linen and towels and clean enough! The bathroom was striking, the tiles were an olive green colour, and it had a vanity unit and a worktop along one side of the room. There was a shower over the bath and the window ledge was spacious. It was well set out, very clean and a decent size for a bathroom. The bedroom was large, although not as big as the room we had in Fowler Road, but that did not put me off in the slightest. The house was fairly new and it was in very good condition.

Beckton was not necessarily a good location for transport it was where the old gas works used to be and the local council had started building in Beckton about 10 years prior to us viewing the house. I fell in love with the house and I was elated when Anthony said he loved it also. We put in an offer which was accepted and we set about getting our first mortgage. It proved difficult for us because Anthony did not earn much money and his wages were paid cash in hand, also I had not been at my current employers, Marks and Spencer's, long enough. No one would give us a mortgage and it seemed like our dream house was slipping away before our eyes. Fortunately we were able to eventually secure a mortgage with the Chelsea Building Society; however, the interest rate was high.

We moved into our new home in the summer using the vans that Anthony and Gerald used for work as removal vans. There was not much to move as we were yet to buy a lot of our own stuff. It took a while to get all the furniture we needed but I did not care because I was so happy that we had finally bought our own home. The freedom was great, I could walk around in my home now without clothes on if I so wished. Anthony built a wall to wall wardrobe in the bedroom at the opposite end of the window, he did a very good job and I was very proud of him.

I enjoyed cooking for my husband although it was not long before I started to find it a bit of a chore. You see Anthony started work very early in the mornings, 6.00am and although I did not get up at that time I often woke up. I then had to get up around 7.00am to get to work for 9.00am. I then finished work at 5.30 whilst Anthony was done around 2.00pm the latest, he would then pick me up at Plaistow station. I would then start the cooking, so it was a very long day for me. There were times when Anthony would have me waiting for him at the station and when he did arrive late there was often no apology and no kiss. This would annoy me very much and I got tired of mentioning it. I felt there was no reason for him to be continually late as he finished work hours before me. He was so miserable when he picked me up and I often thought that he probably resented having to do so.

Work was finally starting to get better for me, after floating I landed a job in the International Foods department after covering for someone's holiday. The staff in the department really liked me and how efficient I was, so much so that they spoke with HR in order to take me on permanently rather than have their old secretary back when she returned from her holiday. I felt a bit sorry for her, however they wanted the best person for the job and it happened to be me. This boosted my confidence. I worked for a team of 11 and they were a lovely bunch of people and I enjoyed working for them. The job was challenging and I had to type out foreign ingredients list on a daily basis as part of my role.

Gill became my best friend at work, we became very close. I was extremely fond of Gill and I looked to her for advice on life and fashion tips. We were entitled to two breaks of 20 minutes and a lunch hour and we so enjoyed meeting up at those times. There was a canteen and I would meet Gill, Wendy, Lorraine and others at these times, often getting carried away having a laugh over coffee, or tea and biscuits and/or cake, sometimes our break times ended up being 30 minutes long. Lunch times were just as fun, we would either go for something to eat and then to the shops or just sit in the canteen for the whole hour and chat and laugh. I would always have dessert, my favourite being treacle sponge and custard. I was enjoying my work life more so than my home life.

I started to feel that something was missing and was not very happy. My niece Mary-Ann was adorable and I loved her dearly. One day it dawned on me that I probably should have my own baby; maybe that would make me feel happier. So I set about to tell Anthony that I thought we should have a baby; however, he was not keen on the idea because we had only been married for just over a year and had a mortgage, he felt we could not afford to have a baby at this time. However, yet again I managed to convince him that it would be fine; I would go back to work after having the baby. He succumbed and it was not long before I fell pregnant, I was six weeks pregnant by the time we found out about it and I was excited about the prospect of being a mum.

My pregnancy was not an easy one, morning sickness and acute tiredness took it out of me. The tiredness was so bad that I would fall asleep at my desk. The doctor suggested that I have a nap at lunch times which my employers agreed to. There was a nurses' station at work with two beds, a bit like a mini hospital ward. I would have my lunch and then sleep for 45 minutes. I slept so deeply, the nurse would have to wake me up at the allotted time. I did not glow one bit, my skin was dreadful and my hair became dry and brittle so I just put it in extensions to give it a break.

I was eager to wear maternity clothes and started wearing them before I really needed to because I just loved the idea of being pregnant even though I felt quite ill with it. I was showing by five months and before long I started to get bigger and bigger which slowed me down. As the summer approached I found it very difficult, my feet swelled up, my thighs were rubbing and I just found the whole experience quite distressing, I was exhausted and felt like a beached whale by the end of my pregnancy.

Work was a struggle so I left to go on maternity leave as soon as it was legally possible, I needed to rest. Looking back now I wish I stayed on for as long as possible, that way I would have been able to stay with my baby longer before going back to work. My work colleagues were so generous. Gill worked for the Baby Department and she contributed many baby clothes, a carrier which was packed with baby toiletry products. My department bought me a bath set and a rocking seat. Everyone's generosity and kindness overwhelmed me.

Anthony had to come and pick me up in the car in order to take me and all our lovely gifts home. I instructed him on what to wear and he wore everything I told him to, a pair of jeans, his blue jeans shirt and his tanned cowboy boots. I wanted everyone to see how gorgeous he was. What a show off I was!

Leaving work filled me with sadness, I enjoyed working in that department and I was going to miss them as well as Gill and my other friends. They all gave me such a good send off and wished me well. Gill and Lorraine helped us down to the car with the presents which were really quite cumbersome. Once Anthony came back with the car they loaded it, we said our goodbyes and off we drove to prepare for our new life as parents.

Chapter 17

Childbirth - 1991

My baby was due on the 2nd September (our anniversary). Unfortunately she did not arrive on time, which by now was causing me distress as I was huge! Around my due date I had a scare because the baby had stopped moving. I panicked and went to the doctor to inform them of my concerns. By now I was worried that my child had died inside me. They did a scan to check for a heartbeat and luckily enough there was a heartbeat, my baby was ok; the relief was insurmountable. I was given a work sheet which I needed in order to record my baby's movements.

I became very anxious that my baby was overdue, it was difficult for me to get around; I had put on around five stones and knew now why people described pregnant women as beached whales, because I certainly felt like one. It became so uncomfortable for me; my feet were swollen and it was a hot summer that year, which did not help me in the slightest.

I became desperate to give birth but nothing was happening, I even got Anthony to assist by having sex to see if that would loosen things up a little. It seemed to work because I started having contractions on Friday 13th September, so off I went with my husband in tow to the hospital ready to have this baby at last. When we arrived I was checked over, and was only 2cm or 3cm dilated. A somewhat rude midwife told me that I needed to go home because I was not in labour. I was furious; I was in pain and my baby was overdue, what did she mean I was not in labour? We returned home only to return again the following day in absolute agony. This time they kept me in even though I was only about 4cm dilated by now. The contractions were painful and I did not know how long I could take this for.

It seemed like eternity, and nothing much was happening, I had managed to progress to 5cm; half way there. I needed pain relief so I chose the gas and air which helped but also made me as high as a kite. I started singing along to the songs on the radio, 'I'm too sexy for my shirt' by Right Said Fred was playing and after singing along I then started to curse the guys who sang the song, then a Madonna song and again I cursed her also. More gas and air was necessary. Hours later and still no more progress down below, loads of gas and air caused me to go into a bit of frenzy; I started crying out for a caesarean, only to be told by the gynaecologist that they don't give caesareans on request. I insisted that I had been in labour for so long and nothing was happening, they had even put me on a drip to help progress the labour yet that did not work.

Eventually, the gynaecologist checked me to see if I had dilated any further, and to my dismay I had not. As I was being checked a horrible feeling swept over me which I could not explain. It felt as if the gynaecologist was being quite unprofessional in the way he was checking me – a bit like a pervert – but I was overwhelmed with the whole situation to even say anything. He finally agreed that I would have to have a caesarean because I was still only 5cm dilated. Damn right, you stupid little man was the thought that came to my mind. Due to my religious beliefs I had to sign a consent form before they operated that they would be exempt if anything happened to me due to the fact that I would not accept a blood transfusion under any circumstances, even death. My husband had to sign also. My mum and mother-in-law both turned up at the hospital looking very worried for me.

By now I was quite delirious and just wanted this baby out. They decided to give me a general anaesthetic – I was pretty wiped out by now and it was the best option. The next thing I remember is being woken up by my husband who handed me my baby; the first thing I said was, "Is it a girl?" to which he replied "Yes". I knew it, I knew I was having a girl and that's exactly what I wanted. I looked at her and thought, oh my beautiful baby girl with her lovely thick jet black hair. Was she really mine? She was born on Sunday 15th September at 11.59am weighing in at a massive 9lb 4oz; no wonder she could not come out naturally! At the suggestion of my granny we called her Naomi.

On examining her we saw that she had two extra half size fingers next to her little fingers. They just flopped around at the side of her hands. Anthony was somewhat pleased to see this because it ran in his family, so he was sure she was his child. I was not impressed with that thinking, because who else's child could it be? The paediatrician said that they would use silk cotton to cut the extra fingers off, they would wrap it round the base of the fingers – which had no bones thankfully – and they would drop off after some days. I wanted to know if it would hurt her and they said it would hurt a little. I found it difficult to accept that my baby had only just started out in life and she would be feeling pain so soon. They took her away, I lay there anxiously waiting and before long I heard my precious baby screaming. My heart jolted and there I was crying for my baby.

I stayed in the hospital with Naomi for 5 days, it was not a nice experience, the hospital was dirty and not all of the staff was pleasant. My stomach was very uncomfortable – I could not even laugh when I wanted to because it was just too painful and it was difficult to breast feed because Naomi was heavy and I could not pick her up. I needed a lot of assistance especially with feeding her because Naomi found it difficult to latch on. There came a point when I nearly gave up breast feeding – ooh the pain – but persevered.

Coming home with my new baby girl was a big occasion. When I arrived home the place was spotless and Anthony had brought me a huge bouquet of flowers and set all the cards we had received around the living room – God bless him – it all looked so welcoming. Motherhood was no easy task; I was constantly tired and irritable. Breast feeding made me permanently hungry, however I desperately needed to lose my baby weight so I tried hard not to eat too much. My craving for orange juice had now subsided which was good because I probably drank a whole river full of it whilst I was pregnant.

About the third day of being at home, Naomi was crying so I tried to feed her, she would not latch onto the breast and so I put her back into her beautifully decorated Moses basket, which was right beside my bed. She continued crying profusely, I tried to comfort her, but she was not having any of it. I became so distressed because of sheer exhaustion and frustration that I shouted into the basket at the top of my voice with so much venom "What's wrong with you?" Anthony came running up the stairs to find out what was wrong and he took her and tried to settle her down. Thank God for that I thought, I desperately needed some sleep and what a way to talk to my baby, I felt so bad.

Anthony was a very attentive father, and we pretty much shared the responsibilities of looking after our daughter. We had many visitors to our home to see the new arrival. I was delighted to see most of them, however, I would not let anyone hold her except for family, and if they did hold her they had to wash their hands first. I was not having her catch anything. Even when we went back to the Kingdom Hall this rule lasted for quite some time. I did not care if people thought I was being particular. Naomi was my baby and I had to protect her.

Chapter 18

Back to Work

Time flew by and before long I had to go back to work; Naomi was only 14 weeks old. I did not want to go back because I enjoyed being a stay at home mum, however, I was the bread winner in the family and my wage was a necessity. I had to wean Naomi off the breast during the daytime so that we could both get use to it, however, this proved very difficult as she would not feed from the bottle during the day. She literally starved herself during the daytime and then guzzled down the breast milk at the end of the day, leaving my nipples very sore, she was on them for what seemed like forever. Stubborn little baby she was! Finally, the day came for me to go back to work and I arranged for her to be looked after by my mother, I was glad that she would be looked after by family, she would be safer than in a nursery (so I thought...) and it would not cost me half as much. Plus she would be company for Mary-Ann her cousin. Mum did not work so I gave her some money for looking after Naomi. When I dropped Naomi off at my mum's I cried all the way to work, it was as if someone took a part of me away, it was one of the most difficult things I had to do.

Being back at work was just awful, I was not able to return to the same department that I had previously worked for due to company policies which meant that secretaries were not guaranteed a job in the same department on their return from maternity leave; outrageous, I thought. After the first week I knew I could not cope with working full time and having a young baby so I asked if I could go part time, which they agreed to. I floated in the Wine department which I enjoyed where I met Natalie. She was a very pretty girl who loved talking just as much as I did. Natalie joined us girls at break and lunch time and we became great friends even till this day. The good thing about working at Marks and Spencer was that you received lots of goodies, and I would get bottles of wine to take home on a weekly basis.

Because of Anthony's hours he would pick Naomi up from my mum's which was handy for me. I did not work Tuesday's and Thursday's and I enjoyed my days off with Naomi, I would take her to baby and toddler groups and do housework on those days, I also tried to cook in advance for the following day just to make my working day easier.

One day whilst changing Naomi's nappy there was a very tiny amount of blood in her nappy. I was very concerned about this and started to panic thinking all sorts. I decided to take her to the doctor, who very casually examined her and said there was nothing really to worry about as it was quite a normal occurrence. This put my mind at ease, however from that day on, Anthony and I found it important to tell Naomi even as a baby to make sure that no-one played with her private parts and if they did she were to tell mummy and daddy. I didn't care if Naomi did not understand what we were saying but felt I had to say this to her regularly and hope that it would sink in somehow.

Working in the Wine Department came to an end because they needed a full time secretary so I transferred to the

Savoury Snacks and Confectionery Department. Yum yum! Even better! It took a while for me to settle in; I worked alongside another assistant a young girl named Alison. We got on really well and worked together as a team; both very efficient. Again, having the goodies was great, not only did I get them to take home; I ate at my desk constantly to get me through the day. It was a large department and also incredibly busy. There were times when they wanted the work yesterday. It was rather difficult for me at times, because I had to leave on time to get home to my daughter. I felt that some members of the department were oblivious to my needs as a young working mother. I had many an argument, in particular with two of my line managers, one I just walked out on because she wanted me to stay behind to finish work which I was not prepared to do because it had been given to me too late in the day. Another occasion I got into an argument with a different manager who then proceeded to tell me, "You have a chip on your shoulder." I was outraged, this horrid little man talking to me in such a fashion. I reported his arse to HR, because if ever there was a racist comment, that was it. I cannot remember the outcome but I was onto him, he was so short and must have been suffering from Napoleon Syndrome! I hated working for them and to be honest I hated the work I did, it was so boring and did not challenge me mentally. It was also difficult working and being a mum; I did not know how much more of this I could take.

Although mum looked after Naomi when I worked, she often moaned about how difficult it was for her, because she also looked after Mary-Ann, and her husband the lazy arse Rick who did not work because he still claimed to have a bad back, so she had to look after him too. I felt under pressure, we had a mortgage to pay, Anthony did not earn much, we had outgrown our home, I did not want to leave my baby with just anyone and I hated my job.

That familiar feeling of depression loomed over me once more. I was not happy with my lot in life, I was finding it all so difficult, but no-one really knew – I swallowed it, like I always did. My weight was increasing which seemed to happen overnight. Living in a larger home was something I dreamed of, but we could not afford to sell, you see the Thatcher era was cracking, England was in the middle of a recession and our property was no longer worth what we had paid for it. What were we to do? There had to be a solution. I thought long and hard about our predicament and came up with a great idea. I put it to Anthony to see what he thought and he agreed because at least it meant that I would not be giving up my job and we would not lose any money on our home.

The solution? We moved back into our first home in Fowler Road, you see, it was only occupied by his mother now. It was a good size three bedroom maisonette, room for Naomi to now have her own room a kitchen large enough for a dining table, it was ideal. My mother-in-law would move into our lovely one bedroom house. It would be perfect for her. She agreed and the deed was done. I was sad to leave our home, because I loved it, but it was no longer practical. We kept the house in our name however; Anthony's mother would pay the mortgage and all the bills direct and vice versa; except we carried on paying the rent for both properties.

Although our new home was not on the ground floor, it was better for a family as there was more room. We set about redecorating it to make it more homely. As is customary Anthony made a built in wardrobe in the main bedroom and a built in cabinet in the living room, naturally he did an excellent job. I was excited about painting Naomi's bedroom and I decorated it in pink and white, I decided to get creative and used stencils with bunnies around the room, making it look pretty for my little girl. I even added a colourful alphabet banner that went around the whole room.

Naomi had by now developed asthma and skin problems, eczema was appearing all over her body; we applied creams and lotions and bathed her in special oils supplied to us by the doctor. They helped a little, but it was distressing for her. One day Naomi's skin flared up, she had boils all over her body. The doctor could not diagnose her. I was becoming extremely worried for my little girl; it was awful seeing her in such distress. We had to take her to see a consultant at the hospital, they said she had scabies. "Scabies?" I didn't think that still existed in this day and age?" My poor little girly; oh how she suffered. There was not much we could do apart from apply the usual creams and wait for it to run its course. She continued to suffer with eczema and asthma, having to use inhalers through a huge plastic tube.

Life at Fowler Road had its pros and cons; it was just five minutes away from my mum so dropping Naomi off to go to work was a dream. Despite having a lot more room; being on the first floor was not very convenient, especially with a little one in tow having to lug her up and down the stairs in her pram was not easy on my back, especially with the extra weight I had to carry myself. My depression was getting worse I was at the GP surgery nearly every week for some stress related illness and it got to the point where I was prescribed antidepressants. I finally had to give up working; it was all too much for me. Anthony and his mother did not seem pleased because it meant my wage was no longer available and they put pressure on me to continue working. I considered my health to be more important, and wished I had made the decision sooner.

Chapter 19

Full Time Mum - 1994

Being a full time mum was a lot easier, apart from having less money, of course. Anthony's mum now had to pay for the rent as well as the mortgage at Partridge Close. I did not feel guilty about this because she was now married to some guy named Peter, who was just as lazy as my own mother's husband. Surely between the two of them they could manage and cover the bills. I became quite resentful that they all wanted me to carry on working just so that my wages could pay for the majority of the bills. What the hell did they take me for?

I had so much more time on my hands, I filled it with housework, going to mother and toddler groups and eating. I continued gaining weight, I tried the slimming world diet and it worked for a while, I managed to lose 1 ½ stones. I tended to do the carbohydrate days more often than the protein days which then led to my weight loss becoming stagnant, so before long I gave up on that diet and the weight plus some came back on. Money was short and I felt a bit disconnected from my husband.

Before long I found being at home quite boring so I found a job working just 12 hours a week for a Professor of Medical Ethics at the London Whitechapel Hospital Medical College. I enjoyed the job, and was grateful to the sister from the congregation who helped me get it – it was a job share. Certain aspects of the job I found challenging because I was asked to do research on certain ethical programmes that came on television. This job was certainly different to my previous ones and I enjoyed it. Life was becoming a little bit more bearable.

My sister was having problems with her marriage and it came to light that her husband was beating her. She had kept this in for about six years. Everyone was shocked, he seemed so gentle. As I thought back to a conversation we had some years ago, "I cannot believe that you can tell Anthony to shut up, I could never say anything like that to Gerald." I did not think anything of it at the time but now it all made sense. Their marriage ended, my sister was a bit of a mess, very vulnerable and trying to make a fresh start, she actually was the one that moved out of the marital home with her daughter; that did not make any sense to me. She needed a lot of support; I tried to give her as much as I could, although I did not feel I was the best candidate for the job because I was not too happy myself.

Things between Anthony and me were steadily becoming worse, in fact his behaviour was somewhat weird and I did not know what was wrong with him. I tried talking to him and asked him if I had done anything to upset him. He assured me it was not me. I could not understand why he was so distracted, emotionally detached from me and clearly distressed about something and I could not bear it. My mother came round to see me one day and asked me how we were. I told her that things were not too good. She then asked me if I ever looked at Gerald or would even consider getting involved with him in any way. 'What a strange question to be asking me,' I thought. I categorically told her, "No way, he's my brother-in-law and that's how I see him". My mother then divulged to me as sensitively as she could, "Charlene and Anthony have been seeing each other."

I immediately went into a state of shock, I could not believe what I was hearing, my head started to hurt, my heart started to crack and I felt as if I was going to go mad. I needed my mum to tell me again just to make sure I heard her right the first time. She repeated herself, "Charlene and Anthony have been seeing each other". Without knowing what I was doing I left the house abruptly, leaving my little girl at home with my mother. I walked the streets of Forest Gate feeling like a mad woman. I went to a phone box and called my aunty Olivia and told her what had just happened, I told her that I would not and could not go back home. I felt so desperate; I just wanted to end my life, yet again. But how could I, Naomi needed me. So what the hell was I supposed to do now? I went to the shops, bought chocolate and I started to feel numb...

I don't know who convinced me to go back home, but I did. I guess it had something to do with the fact that I had a child to look after. When Anthony and I finally spoke about the events, he explained that he was very sorry and he did not know why he did it. I needed details, times, places, days, everything. When he finished telling me all that he was prepared to tell me; which was not everything, I mustered all the strength I had in me and thumped him in his head, he later said that he saw stars. He allowed me that privilege of thumping him, although it did not make me feel much better. I felt as if my whole world was falling apart.

I was still in shock about the whole debacle and could not believe that my husband and my sister would both betray me in this way. What on earth were they thinking? I started to feel very disconnected with life and everyone around me; I was drifting along aimlessly, too scared to feel the pain and the following day in the afternoon I took an overdose of paracetamol. Anthony came home from work only to see me passed out on the sofa with poor little Naomi wondering what had happened to her mum. Everything was hazy and I was in and out of consciousness. Anthony called my mother and an ambulance. The paramedics took me into the ambulance with my mum coming along and Anthony driving closely behind with Naomi in tow. The hospital staff pumped my stomach. I saw a doctor, but could not and did not want to talk so I was given some information on counselling services that were available.

I did not seek the services that were on offer. The elders of the congregation were informed and they counselled us, Anthony was reprimanded and encouraged to make amends to me. They also informed me that as adultery had not really taken place If I chose to leave him I would not be able to divorce and remarry in the eyes of the Lord, so I was encouraged to find it in my heart to forgive him. What a load of twat! I was sure there was a scripture that said if you so look at another woman in that way you have already committed adultery with her in your heart. After some days I was able to talk more freely to him, he assured me that they really did not go all the way. So I insisted that he start to communicate more with me and treat me like his queen if I was to forgive him and we were to continue with the marriage. He agreed to my requests.

Things were never the same again! The love I had for Anthony started to fade, I could not cope with what he had done, and it bugged me so much; I could not find any peace.

But I could not leave him. I had stopped talking to my sister, although I was very angry with her I felt as if I had lost her and I missed her. She went to live in New York because she could not bear the thought of me not talking to her. She stayed for five years. Some years later whilst she was in New York and I could handle talking to her we spoke on the phone; I could see how sorry she was and I forgave her.

Chapter 20

Second Baby - 1995

I was in the depths of depression, and I needed something to distract me. I had the solution, another baby, a companion for Naomi. Anthony was not keen on the idea, we were already struggling, I did not care; I just wanted another baby. I stopped using contraception and after a few months I fell pregnant for the second time. Once again I felt like I had some purpose.

My second pregnancy was different from the first, I did not feel so tired, I glowed a lot more and my hair seemed to flourish and shine unlike before. I was concerned about my iron, as it was low and I had to take iron tablets, I also drank Guinness mixed with nutriment to keep my iron levels up plus it tasted good! I was completely oblivious to the fact that Guinness was alcohol. I ate less during this pregnancy because I did not want another huge baby and did not want to put on as much weight as I did the first time. I had to have a diabetes check because my first baby was so large to rule out a diabetic pregnancy, which is one reason for large babies. Thankfully that turned out fine and I did not develop diabetes due to pregnancy.

Although I worked such small hours, I had to climb three flights of stairs to get to my office and found it extremely difficult the larger I became, to be honest those flights of stairs were a chore even without being pregnant. I needed to take a long breather after each flight; it probably took me 10 minutes to get to the top! The toilets were two flights down from my office so I even held onto my wee for far too long at times just so I would not have to climb back up the stairs. Boy was I glad I only had to go into the office twice a week.

My baby was due on June 9th 1995. I was excited as well as stressed. I left work quite soon because I did not plan to return since I had not been with them long enough to be entitled to maternity leave, besides they were quite upset that I had fallen pregnant so soon after taking the job, which I thought was a bleeding cheek. 'How can employers dictate to you when you should plan for a child?' were my sentiments. Mind you it was the other secretaries/congregation sisters that were more concerned than my boss, 'Bleeding busy bodies,' I thought.

Once I left work I started getting the nursery ready. The spare room had been packed with items that had no real home. Clearing it out was a task and a half. We decided to decorate it with lemon, light green and white. The walls were painted lemon with an accent wall; green and white striped patterned wallpaper. I made the curtain from green and white striped material which matched the wallpaper nicely and the carpet was a light green. The nursery was bright and cheerful, just right for a baby.

When my due date had arrived and no sign of labour I was disappointed – I could not go through being two weeks overdue like before. I decided to go for long walks to help baby out, I was surprised at the speed at which I found myself walking. I took castor oil; it was absolutely disgusting to drink, it felt like I was drinking slime. After taking it and walking over to my grandmother's house in Manor Park the first signs of labour started to appear.

I had booked to have my second baby at the London Whitechapel Hospital this time round and was seeing a very well known gynaecologist by the name of Wendy Savage, who was not keen on caesareans. She was brilliant; she wanted to do her very best for me so that I could have a normal birth on this occasion. At my earlier appointments we discussed pain relief and the possibility of having an epidural so that I could be awake for the birth if indeed I had to have a caesarean.

Contractions were coming through thick and fast and I decided it was time to go to the hospital, we called to let them know how often the contractions were coming and they agreed that I should come in. Anthony drove me to the hospital. I also called my friend Gill who agreed to be one of my birthing partners. By the time I arrived at the hospital I was in agony and hoped with all my might that my labour would not last as long as the first one. A good sign was that they did not have to break my waters, they broke by themselves and it was a horrible green colour, quite embarrassing really. Even though my waters had broken, I was still not dilating very much. My gynaecologist was not at the hospital, but she was called out and she was advising her staff over the phone, this made me feel quite special, she really cared.

I had the epidural which really took care of the pain. I was being checked by a male doctor who thought it quite funny to say "What would you say if I told you that your baby has black curly hair?" I did not find it amusing one little bit; there I was flat on my back, feet in stirrups with my privates out of doors for all and sundry to see and this doctor thinks it is appropriate to crack jokes. I hated being checked, it was humiliating and painful; kicking the doctor in his mouth suddenly seemed plausible! 'Why do men become gynaecologists?' I thought to myself. My labour dragged on and I did not dilate any more than five centimetres, just like before. Gill had arrived and she was a welcome sight, she helped me see the funny side of things despite the fact that I was distressed and tired. My mother and mother-in-law also arrived at the hospital both looking worried just like they did when Naomi was born.

Things started to take a turn for the worse; my baby was going into distress – Hello! So was I; and there were no signs of me dilating any further. Wendy Savage authorised a caesarean over the phone and the epidural was topped up. Anthony and Gill had to wear these special gowns and masks in order to be present. I was disappointed that I could not have the baby naturally, but was glad that my labour would be over soon. The staff painted iodine on my abdomen before cutting me open, I could feel some sort of sensation but no real pain, it was weird. Anthony was holding my hand and Gillian was at the other end ready with her camera. There was a lot of tugging going on and that also felt quite strange, the baby's arm flew out first and they had to put it back inside and search for its head in order for it to come out first. The head was stuck in my pelvis so it was difficult for them to get it out. Finally they managed to do so and the rest is history. It was a boy! He was born on the 15th June 1995. He weighed in at 9lb exactly, which I was pleased about because it was 4oz smaller than Naomi. One of each, 'No need to do this ever again,' I thought.

They had to take him away for a while just to make sure that everything was ok with him. Before long he was wrapped up and given to me by Anthony after I was stitched up. He was gorgeous, his little face was all screwed up with these little spots dotted around it and his hair was jet black with loose curls. We called him Adrian which was one of his granddad's names. Wendy Savage had arrived by now and she came to see how I was, she apologised for not being there and said "Sorry you had to have the caesarean, we did all we could." I found it odd how she was such a professional person yet still so caring, I did not think the two would fit together, but obviously it did in her case.

My stay at Whitechapel hospital was far nicer than that of Newham. I had my own room for a start and the nurses were a lot more sympathetic and helpful. The day after the birth I was given a bed bath, something I found quite embarrassing. The following day I was told that I had to get up and start walking around, I was petrified; I was still in so much pain and the thought of moving just seemed impossible. However I did as they said and managed, with the nurses help, to get up, move around and even wash myself.

It was after five days that I was able to return home with my son, it was good to be home. The house was spotless; his Moses basket looked very inviting with new white covers which I had made to spruce it up a bit. Naomi was excited to have her little brother and there was not much jealousy on her side, I had prepared her for his arrival ever since I started to show and she knew she was still mummy's little girl. She was very helpful, fetching and carrying things to make life easier.

Now, Anthony and his family were from Sierra Leone which meant that Adrian had to be circumcised. "Over my dead body," I stressed. Anthony and his mother tried convincing me by saying that he would never get infections and changing his nappies would be easier for me. I finally succumbed and on his

9th day of being alive my baby boy was circumcised. Even though I had agreed to this I was terrified for him. I wanted to know exactly what happens and what pain killers will be used and whether he would be given a local anaesthetic. When they told me that he would not be given an anaesthetic I was horrified. 'How evil,' I thought. 'How can they do that to a baby?' I wanted to change my mind, however, it was all booked and after all it was part of their culture.

I anxiously waited outside whilst Anthony and his mum went in with Adrian, I couldn't bear to see my baby go through this pain, it reminded me of when Naomi had her extra fingers tied so that they would fall off. It was a Jewish Rabbi that performed the circumcision in what he called his office come surgery. I was really quite apprehensive about the whole thing even though I was constantly assured that everything would be ok. As I waited outside nervously, suddenly I heard a scream and then hysterical crying from my baby boy. I instantly started to cry and wanted to comfort him. Minutes later they appeared with Adrian still crying and in distress. I immediately put him on the breast to help comfort him and before no time had passed he fell asleep. He slept for the best part of that day; my poor little mite. His little willy had a small white bandage tied round the end of it; Anthony and his mum took on the role of changing Adrian's nappies until he healed since I certainly could not face doing it.

By this time Adrian also had developed eczema pretty badly, much worse than Naomi's. He also had bronco spasms which is similar to having constant asthma attacks. We were in and out of hospital with him and we became familiar faces at the Children's Hospital in Hackney which has sadly now closed down. Staff members were very fond of Adrian over the years as he was quite a cheerful but cheeky character.

Adrian's eczema and asthma were acute and Naomi's was still bothering her. Adrian would just sit and scratch constantly, it was painful to watch as he would scratch till his skin was red raw and bleeding. I had to change his clothes three times daily because he produced so much dead skin which would just irritate him even more. One night I put socks on his hands to stop him from scratching until he bled, I put elastic bands round the wrists so the socks would not fall off. In the morning I was shocked when one of his hands had doubled in size; the elastic band was too tight. I felt awful, like I was a cruel mother, but it was an accident, I just could not bear to see him scratching the way he did, it was heart breaking.

We lived across the road from a bird seed factory which created a lot of dust in the local area, where loads of pigeons would gather around looking for food. It was a health hazard and definitely exacerbated my children's illness. We tried to get a transfer with the council and it proved very difficult. We even visited our local MP Tony Banks in order to help us out with getting this transfer. We had months of visits to our local housing office, getting doctors letters and phone calls trying to deal with this issue which proved very stressful. I also struggled with getting Naomi to nursery every day because we lived on the top floor of a block of maisonettes which meant me lugging down the buggy and Adrian with Naomi in tow. I had started out using a baby sling, however, Adrian was a heavy baby and my back could no longer take the strain.

Anthony decided to jack in his job and go to university. He said he needed to be able to get a better job in order to provide properly for his family. I was a little scared for financial reasons at first, but then realised it was a good decision and was proud that he made that decision. Life was tough, because he was studying by day and working at Burger King by night. He did not have much time for me or the kids and I was busy being a full time mum and wife. I suggested to Anthony that he give up the job and we apply for income support, I thought we would be better off and he would not be so tired and would have more time for the kids and me. However, he enjoyed his job and did not give it up.

I would take my children to mother and toddler group. There was one such group at our local McDonalds Restaurant in Woodgrange Road. Our small fee included unlimited coffee and a doughnut. I looked forward to this because my friends Michelle and Georgia also attended; Georgia's kids were already in school, but she was a child minder. We made friends with other mothers and child minders as well as Vee the staff member in charge of the group. The kids would play whilst we exchanged baby stories. I also loved the fact that a free doughnut was included in the price, I always chose the cinnamon flavour and most weeks would buy another after having to share my one with the kids. Some weeks we would stay for lunch and other times I would go back to Georgia's for lunch or she would come to mine.

Chapter 21

Degradation Revisited - 1996

I would sometimes visit my mum's during the week, she had moved now to a house in East Ham opposite Central Park School. She had a garden so it was good for the kids to run around and play. One particular day I was in the kitchen with my mum, Adrian was asleep on the sofa. Naomi was in the living room with Rick. As I approached the door to go into the living room I heard Naomi shout out "No" to Rick. She said it quite loudly, so when I opened the door I asked him "What did she do?" assuming she was being naughty. He replied, "Oh nothing," looking very suspicious. I did not like the atmosphere in the room, but just kept the feeling to myself for a while.

I had felt very unnerved by what happened and I don't know why, I started to think all sorts and even wondered if he had interfered with my daughter, but it was not much to really go on. I asked Naomi's nursery teacher if it was easy for her to spot a child that had been abused. She told me that she could spot them because children who were abused would normally be quite insular and withdrawn. I then asked her if she thought Naomi was, however, she did not think so because she saw Naomi as a confident and happy child. I was a little perplexed, but then she added, "But follow your gut instinct." Those words rang loudly in my ears.

So I did and kept a watchful eye on my little girl. One day when I was bathing my babies Naomi was asking me questions about his little penis, she seemed overly curious about it. So I very casually asked her if she had seen any other penises before. To my surprise she said she had. I started to fret but not wanting to frighten or alarm her in the softest, kindest voice I could muster up I said, "Really? Whose?" and she responded, "Rick's". Horrified and confused, my head started to race and I wanted to throw up, but I needed to be sure so again I asked her in that same soft voice, "And what did his penis look like?" She responded "It was all pink and crinkly." Pink and crinkly, pink and crinkly. Those words will haunt me until I die! I hurriedly got them out of the bath, left the room, burst into tears and quickly ran to Anthony to tell him what I had just found out.

He was so cool and collected it made me sick. I did not see any emotion, maybe it was just disbelief he was showing. I ran through the whole scene that I had just had with Naomi with him, so he knew what I was talking about. We called the police, my mum, his mum and my grandmother. Social services, child protection all got involved. It was a living nightmare! Naomi was checked over at the hospital, she was interviewed which was recorded so she would only have to go through the ordeal once. Rick had told her that if she told anyone he would shoot her with his air gun which he possessed and kept in the garden.

Words cannot express the pain I felt for my little girl, I did not protect her from this evil man with his perverted ways. I started to feel guilty and stupid that I had started to trust him when in the beginning I always thought there was something sinister about him. Needless to say, my mum left him. Crown Prosecution could not prosecute because it was her word against his and there were some discrepancies in her statement. Her medical check also showed no signs which could have been because she had not long returned from Washington where she had gone for two weeks with her grandmother (her dad's mum). All Anthony's mum could remember was Naomi complaining about a stick hurting her.

I was dumbstruck when they told us that they were not prosecuting, how could they expect a three year old to give a solid statement? I felt as if my world was falling apart. My poor little girl. Our GP referred us to Child and Family Psychotherapy. We were to go as a family to help us deal with this tragedy. Anthony came once or twice, his excuse was work. I did not take kindly to his decision; however I continued to go as it was for the good of my daughter. One good thing that came out of this was that we were able to move house, we told the council that we saw Rick hanging around outside our home. They moved us to a place in Plaistow within a week or two.

Chapter 22

Upheaval & Turmoil

It was another maisonette although this one was on the ground floor. When we walked in to view it, I was not sure whether I liked it or not. It was mainly due to the décor, it was quite ghastly. It was shoddily done and the colours were so dark and depressing, all the skirting boards were red. The house smelt and there were bits of food on some of the walls. I thought about what sort of people could live like this, and I concluded, nasty ones. However, I tried to remain objective and think about how we could make the house into a home. The hallway was about 50 feet and the living room came off the hallway to the left, it was a large enough room, with a huge window, and a fireplace on the far side of the room, the floor tiles were dark brown and the room looked dismal. The kitchen looked a little better as they had fitted new cabinets in their usual plain white style. They had also fitted new cream tiles so apart from the walls and the pantry it looked quite presentable.

There was a small utility room on from the kitchen which led to the small garden at the back of the house. Beyond the garden was a communal area for all residents to use. Upstairs were three bedrooms the single bedrooms were small and there was an alcove in the master bedroom which gave the room some character. Even though the bathroom was very small, not much space to swing a cat, the suite had been replaced so it was brand new and sparkled in the light. The landing was huge; big enough to house a bookcase or even a computer. Even though the house was in an awful state we felt it was a good enough size and we could see the potential so we decided to accept it.

Moving in was a nightmare, we seemed to have accumulated so much stuff over the last few years. We discovered that the heating was not working, which meant we had no hot water in the middle of winter with two small children. We had to go to my grandmothers to get a bath it was so inconvenient. I was livid and was constantly on the phone to the council for them to sort it out. It took a few visits before they finally fixed the problem which ended up with them putting in a new boiler. Finally having our own hot water and heating was such a welcome treat.

Anthony had not long put in a new kitchen in Fowler Road, so we decided to take them down and use them in the new home. It was a good idea, but it meant the kitchen was in chaos for a few weeks whilst he fitted it at the weekends. I thought I was going to go mad with the house in such disarray. Naomi's bedroom was decorated as soon as possible whereas Adrian's did not get done since we stored a lot of our junk in his room. He slept in our room as he still needed to be close to us due to his illnesses. However, I did not believe in having babies in your bed so I made up a bed for him on the floor with loads of cushions and pillows to protect him. I don't know how, but he always ended up half way across the bedroom which upset me because it meant he was probably cold throughout the night.

We finally got the house decorated and in order within 6 months. We used laminated flooring in the kids' bedrooms, the hallway and the living room in order to eliminate dust, hoping that this would calm down their eczema and asthma. This did help along with all the different remedies we tried such as homeopathy and then finally Chinese herbs which miraculously got rid of the eczema. It was such a relief to see my little boy no longer suffering.

I was now 27 years old and Adrian was about five months, I had problems with contraceptives – weight gain being the major problem. Anthony and I discussed this and we both were not keen on condoms. We discussed sterilisation because we were sure we did not want any more children. I thought it only fair that Anthony have the operation because it would be quicker and easier plus the thought of going under the knife again did not bode well with me. However, he was not willing in the slightest. So because I was absolutely adamant that I could not put by body through another caesarean and I knew that I could not cope with anymore children I felt I had no choice but to have the operation.

It was a tough job convincing the Consultant that I was absolutely sure about this decision. They even asked me to think about what I would do if my kids, god forbids, died or my marriage broke up and I met someone else and wanted to have children with them. Despite those scenarios I was able to convince the Consultant that I was 100% sure even at the tender age of 27. The operation was successfully done through keyhole surgery. Luckily it was not as painful as the caesarean and I was given the option of staying in hospital for an extra night if I wanted, which I did, however Anthony convinced me that he thought it would be better that I come home and he would take care of me.

I decided to come home, being convinced that it was the best thing for me and the children, especially as Adrian was still being breast fed. The following morning Anthony made the breakfast for the kids took Naomi to nursery and off he went to university leaving me with Adrian. I was dumbstruck. He promised I would be better off at home and he would take care of me, it felt as if he just wanted me home to take care of Adrian so he could go off to university. I had to call my mum to come over and help me which she did. I clocked up resentment against Anthony; I felt he was selfish beyond words. I hated him, and I could not stop thinking about what he had done to me in the past with my sister.

I was finding life difficult coping with a young family and a husband who was hardly around due to studying and working. I was eating constantly, practically every hour on the hour which depressed me. I went to the GP; I always seemed to be there, I started to feel like a hypochondriac. I was put on antidepressants again, as well as being signed up for the GP referral scheme at my local gym.

Going to the gym, I was assigned a case worker who was pretty much like a personal trainer helping overweight people to get fit and into a good routine. This helped me somewhat, I managed to lose a bit of weight, I enjoyed the exercise and it wasn't long before I was fit enough to go it alone.

Anthony was busy going to university and working nights and I hardly saw him apart from when we had to go to the Kingdom Hall or out preaching. We did not do anything nice together. I was bored and I found myself a one day a week job at Standard Bank in London as a filing clerk, it got me out of the house and brought in a little spending money.

I hated the nights because most nights Anthony was at work. When he came home I would often be fast asleep. A couple of times I was woken up with him on top of me and inside me, it was a weird feeling and I just let him get on with it until I finally felt like joining in myself. There were times when he wanted us to do certain things which I did not want to do because I found it degrading and demoralising but he did not care, convinced me that there was nothing wrong with it and did it anyway which ended up with me crying quietly into my pillow. It was awful, I felt ashamed and completely used and abused. After two or three times I managed to find the courage to tell him that I would no longer allow that kind of sex again because of how it made me feel. He decided not to protest.

Chapter 23

Counselling Begins

I was attending my counselling sessions with Naomi and they decided it was best if she had her own counsellor. Naomi was not happy with this and she would often try and get out of her session and try to disrupt mine. She was a little tyrant, although I found it quite funny. Adrian was with me, which probably made Naomi jealous; he would sit and play with the toys in the room.

My counsellor was a trained psychotherapist named Mary. She was a middle aged white woman quite tall and slim with thick brown wavy hair. She spoke so quietly and softly which was such a contrast to my voice. She was a nice woman, despite this, it still took a while for me to feel comfortable opening up to her. Some of the sessions I would just sit there and not say much until the last 10-15 minutes of the session when I knew that there would not be enough time to discuss much.

I originally attended counselling to deal with what had happened to my daughter, but somehow it started to lead into my own issues. I found counselling quite painful most of the time having to delve into my past. I did not realise how much my past had affected my present day. I talked about my step dad and how he emotionally abused, teased and treated me as the family scapegoat. I also talked about how my real dad was not around for me when I was growing up, it was all very agonizing. I was very unaware of how much pain I was still carrying around with me.

I started to feel like an emotional wreck; the counselling was bringing up too much painful stuff. I was really starting to hate my life; I missed a lot of meetings at the Kingdom Hall and could not find the energy to even go out preaching. I felt as if Anthony and I were becoming more and more distant, I was struggling with the children and trying to deal with my issues, depression and weight. Things got so bad for me that I finally had a mental breakdown, although at the time I did not realise that's what it was. I did not know what was happening to me, I just could not cope with anything or anyone. My soul had left my body; a feeling I found difficult to explain to anyone.

Adrian was two years old by now and no matter how hard I tried I could not get my life back on track. The elders came round and talked to me to see if they could help, but they could not. The only person that I could really talk to was Mary and that was only once a week. Gill was also a good source of support for me as she always offered a listening ear, just as I did for her. I started talking to her and others such as Georgia about how I could not stand my life. Anthony hated me talking to them and was not afraid to let me know this. Nevertheless, I did not care how he felt about me talking to my friends, at least they were there for me. I was starting to feel that our marriage was over a long time ago, things just were not the same and as much as I tried, there just wasn't much communication or intimacy. Deep in my heart I knew it was over.

Chapter 24

Getting Out - 1997

When Adrian was born we had taken some professional photos with Olan Mills, I had a special makeover picture done, but we could only afford to buy one of those pictures, I loved it. I wore red and my hair was up, I was very happy with that picture and people who came to the house always commented on how lovely I looked. When I needed a boost in confidence, which was very often now I would look at the picture. One day Anthony and I had another argument, he did not want me going out or something and he tried making me feel horrible about myself and in his rage he approached the fireplace, picked up the picture of me, broke the frame and ripped the picture to pieces. I was flabbergasted, but he hadn't finished, he proceeded to move towards me and held my head and started stuffing pieces of the picture into my mouth at the same time telling me, "You think your nice, but you're not all that." I went numb because I could not believe what I had just witnessed.

One day I decided to meet Gill down in the West End for a drink and a chat, I deserved an evening out. We met up at Corks in Binney Street, opposite Selfridges. It was a wine bar by day and a club by night. We arrived in time for happy hour and we ordered all our drinks at the same time to save on costs. We both had a glass of wine and then three bottles of K cider each. The drinks were going down well and we were having a laugh even though I was moaning about my life and my unhappy marriage. I longed for a freer life, the drink was doing a good job of making me feel better and after a while I felt quite jovial. We spoke to a few guys; well they spoke to us! One guy seemed very keen to talk to me, his name was Damian, he was a short dark, thick set guy, fairly cute and we talked a bit and had a dance. By now, not used to drinking so much, I was rather intoxicated, and another guy started teasing us about the way we were dancing, as if we were not doing it properly; well I was but Damien was having difficulty. So I decided to dance with this other guy in a very provocative way, a bit like a tart really, this in some way infuriated Damian. I felt a little bad and ran after him to apologise for my behaviour, although I did enjoy dancing with the other guy. I loved the attention.

I was pretty much legless and needed to get home to the kids, Gill was worried about how I would get home. Damian offered to take me half way, which was very kind of him. I promised Gill that I would call her when I got home so she would know I arrived safely. We all set off for the underground at Bond Street tube and proceeded towards Oxford Circus on the central line. We got off and walked to the Bakerloo line trying to hide our drunken demeanour. Gill went off in the northbound direction and Damian and I in the southbound direction. I needed to get to Embankment on the District line and Damian kindly walked me to the platform where we waited for my train. As we waited we somehow just started kissing, and I felt alive. He took my number and made sure I got onto the train safely.

That was the start of my new life. Anthony and I were arguing especially when I spent time on the phone with my friends. On one occasion he grabbed my mobile phone (yes I was privileged enough to have one back then) and threw it down the toilet. I was in the middle of a conversation, anger engulfed me. I did not want to be married anymore; it was a long time coming. I was in a very confused state and did not know what to do, I spoke to Anthony about wanting to end the marriage, but it fell on deaf ears, as if what I wanted was not important.

One weekend I just picked up an overnight bag and went over to Gill's in Wembley. I was in tears because of our constant arguing and him not accepting that the marriage was over. He was on the phone to me and I just did not know what to say to him, Gillian tried speaking to him, but he just wanted me to come back home, which I did because I felt guilty about leaving the kids behind.

Even though I went back home I was still adamant that the marriage was over and I could not settle. I started going clubbing mainly to Corks wine bar on a Friday. I was very excited about going out because I had forgotten how much I loved dancing; I felt so free and really enjoyed myself. Each time I would drink quite a lot of alcohol, K cider being my favourite. Three bottles was all it took for me to get drunk, blot out the world and my problems.

I realised that I did not have the appropriate clothes for clubbing; most of my clothes were far too decent, so I started buying clothes that were fit for the occasion. One such outfit was a black cat suit which showed quite a bit of cleavage, I loved it and I was not bothered that I was perhaps too overweight to be wearing such a figure hugging garment. I was getting myself ready for a night out, thrilled at the prospect of wearing my new sexy outfit. Anthony was not happy, to say the least, that I was going out clubbing and an argument ensued; our worst ever. I did not want to argue in front of the children because they were getting upset and I constantly told him to stop shouting in front of them, but he could not control his anger. He was so angry that he got my outfit and told me that I did not even have the right shape to be wearing such an outfit and he ripped it to pieces in front of me. I was absolutely livid, my brand new outfit ripped to shreds, I would never forgive him for that.

I could not take any more of his outbursts just because I would not conform to what he wanted. Besides when was he going to get the message that it was over? I packed my bags and left, I went to stay with my grandmother in Warwick Road (my dad's mum). She was happy to have me, her house was still very 70's and it was cold, however I was glad to get away from Anthony and the constant arguing. Nevertheless, I felt unsettled there, it was not home and I was missing my children so I returned home once again after a few days. This I did a couple more times, back and forth. Each time I realised that I missed my children and my home.

Chapter 25

Breaking Up

I was working at Morgan Stanley as a temp at this point, the job was part time, I started at 10.00am and finished at 2.00pm in time to drop Naomi to school and pick her up. However, in a couple of weeks I was due to start doing full time hours. Adrian was being looked after by one of Anthony's family members, she lived in Walthamstow.

I had met up with Damian a few times and we had meals together and went to the cinema. He was ok to pass the time with, a little younger than myself and not really doing much with his life. I even slept with him once, but I got the feeling he was just after my money – not that I had any – wanting to be looked after by an older woman. He wanted to borrow money from me even though I always paid when we went out. He suddenly went down in my estimation, so I decided to stop seeing him. He found it hard to accept and was quite persistent in calling me, but I knew that I wanted nothing more to do with him.

One evening I got home from work, I prepared dinner for the kids and went upstairs to call Gill and update her on Damian. I was engrossed in the conversation and told her everything. The conversation came to an end and I sat on the bed for a while, then unexpectedly I heard this shuffling noise coming from under the bed, it scared the shit out of me and I wondered what it was until I was shocked to see Anthony coming out from under the bed; he heard everything I had said. Needless to say, we had the mother of all arguments. I was shocked that he would stoop so low and spy on me in this way, apparently it was advice he had taken from his mother. He could not believe that I had actually slept with Damian, but I had already told him that the marriage was over even though he would not accept it. 'Besides maybe now you have an idea of how I felt when you fucked about with my own sister,' I thought.

Things became very heated the children were crying, he ripped the gold rope chain that my dad had bought me when I was 16 off my neck; he head butted me and spat in my face. I stayed as calm as I could, nothing he did could hurt me anymore; I did not retaliate, but instead just called the police, I had had enough of this. He called his mother, I called mine. They turned up pretty quickly and my mum arrived with my uncle Len. They tried to calm Anthony down, which was quite a task. The police advised him to leave as it was quite clear that he could not stay in the present circumstances. He was reluctant to leave, but he had no choice because I certainly wasn't leaving this time, one thing for sure was that I wanted to be with my children. So he packed a few things whilst I tried to console the children, most of it was a blur; I just wanted this whole thing to be over.

He took the car and the following morning I had to call work and tell them that I could not come in because I was sick. The weekend came and I tried talking to Anthony to ask him to bring the car back, because I needed it for the children. But he would not oblige; he said he was keeping it. This made me determined to make things work for me and my children, I could see that he was trying to make things difficult. I had just started working longer hours which was good for me financially.

I decided that I would just have to get up earlier and get on the bus with the children. We left the house at 7.00am in the morning and took the 58 bus all the way to Walthamstow and dropped Adrian off at the child minder, after which Naomi and I took the same bus back to East Ham where I dropped her off to Central Park School for around 9.00am. Then I made my way to work in Canary Wharf, by which time I felt as if I had already done a whole days work. At 5.00pm I had to do the journey all over again in reverse, although picking Naomi up from Jackie, the child minder who also had a daughter at the same school. We would arrive home around 8.00pm at which point I would then make dinner, spend a little time with the children, give them their bath and put them to bed. By the end of the day I was absolutely shattered.

This went on for two weeks which caused me to lose weight without even trying. This pleased me. One evening as we got off the bus at Upton Park I saw the family car parked nearby. It was pelting down with rain and we took shelter in the tube station whilst I called Anthony, he did not answer his phone, so I left a message for him to meet me by the car so that he could drop me and his children home. He was not happy to do this, but he had no choice, I had no umbrella to protect them from the rain. I asked him again to let me have the car for the sake of the children and told him how much time they had to spend on the bus and how early I had to wake them up, but he was just not interested. He was keeping the car and that was that. I could not believe how selfish he was being.

In the end I gave up the job, it was too much for me to cope with the break up, the bus journeys and looking after the kids. I informed work about my predicament, and they were sympathetic. I was not happy to give up that job, because I really enjoyed what I was doing, however, they were not prepared to have me go back to the part time hours that I originally had because the department was growing and becoming busier.

Sometime after, I managed to rustle up a few quid and bought a cheap Ford fiesta, it was white and not in very good condition, but it had MOT, a few months tax and it worked. I had my independence once more.

Chapter 26

Single Parent

I tried to put in place times for Anthony to see the children and suggested that he have them every other weekend. He said he would have them when he felt like it. I was not having any of that, I told him that was out of the question as children do not understand "When you feel like it." I told him that he would have them every other weekend or not at all as they needed consistency in order to feel secure. He finally agreed to that and also had them on Tuesday and Thursday evenings because he wanted to continue taking them to the Kingdom Hall, which I had no problem with. He was very consistent with having them and I was pleased about that because they were hardly ever let down by him which was good for them.

Life as a single parent was not easy. I was now on benefits and attending counselling regularly. I tried to have a routine for myself which involved going to aerobics in the mornings, putting Adrian in the crèche. I enjoyed aerobics, it helped keep the weight down and I trained nearly every day including a couple of evenings a week and on Sunday's. Dave also known as The Undertaker was my favourite fitness instructor, his classes were pretty hard core, and I was hooked on his classes like everybody else who took part. During the school holidays, I still went to aerobics, even though Naomi was not allowed in the crèche, so I would let her sit in the class until I finished, quite a few mothers did the same. Even in the evenings I did the same with Adrian although it was a little stressful because it was hard for him to sit still, but this did not stop me from attending my classes.

Some time had passed and I managed to get a loan out to buy my granddad's car the white two-door BMW, because he and my grandmother were immigrating to Jamaica. So I sold the small fiesta that I had not long had for £200.

One day I was driving down the A13 and unfortunately, I had an accident, someone had gone into my car from behind; it was an old car but in good condition and only the boot was damaged. Luckily no-one got hurt. The insurers wrote it off and offered me just over £1,000 for it £100 more than I had paid for it; I took the money and kept the car. I decided to use the money to take the children on holiday. I found a cheap last minute all inclusive holiday to Tunisia. It meant taking Naomi out of school for a week but it was a much needed holiday and the school authorised it.

The flight was four hours long and the kids, especially Adrian were apprehensive about flying because it was his first time on a plane. I found it a little difficult trying to keep them calm, so a couple of drinks from the trolley were in order. We got there in one piece and the hotel was fabulous, it was a four star hotel on the beach.

Our room was beautiful and we enjoyed our days on the beach, in the sea or in the pool. The kids loved it. I put them in the kids clubs so that they could take part in the fun filled activities and mix with the other children. This gave me some much needed time to myself which I would use to relax in the sun, go shopping on the complex or get a massage. I booked myself a massage; however, I was a little nervous about having one and decided to have a triple vodka and tonic before my appointment. Needless to say, I was a little tipsy on arrival. The masseur was a thick set guy who in my opinion was quite unprofessional and far too intimate complementing me on my body. I found it a little difficult to tell him that I thought he was behaving in an unprofessional manner. Besides, the drink made me giggly and deep down I was enjoying the attention. The massage was very relaxing and he did a good job.

After the massage the masseur urged me to come and see him. I agreed and once the kids were in the club I took myself off to see him. It was obvious he wanted sex, and I thought I may as well seeing as I was on holiday and that's what people do when they go away. Isn't it? We were in a shower room with nowhere to really do the deed, so I took out a condom and gave it to him to put on and I turned round and bent over. 'How very unromantic,' I thought. I did not know what was going on behind me but the condom fell on the floor. I was none too pleased; I didn't have condoms to waste. I took out another one and gave it to him, again he was struggling, at which point I turned round to see what his problem was. It was clear to spot (well not that clear); his penis was the size of my little finger, and that is not an exaggeration, it was no wonder the condom fell off. When I saw it, my instant reaction was one of complete and utter horror and the bitch in me laughed and said, "Is that it?" To which he replied, "No, no, you rub and it get big," in his Arabic accent. My response was "Hell no," and off I went in a huff half disappointed and laughing at what I had just seen. 'What did he think he could do with that?' I wondered.

Each time I passed the massage parlour he would call out to me asking if I wanted another massage. I knew what he really wanted; my kids on the other hand, did not. They would shout out to him "No she does not want a massage." I found it quite funny because little did they know what he really meant!

One lunch time I spotted a chef that I took a fancy to; he was tall and fresh faced, very handsome. I gave him the eye and before long he came over to our table and arranged for us to meet up. It was as simple as that, we met up and got to know each other a little, I found him to be quite a sweet guy. We went to a club and walked on the beach and talked. I even met him during the day when I had the children and was kissing him in front of them, very bad behaviour. One night we tried having sex on the beach but the sand kept giving way underneath us and it was not working out, shame because he was well endowed, unlike the masseur!

I made friends with people at the hotel when we all met up for the evening entertainment. It's amazing how nice people are when on holiday in a relaxed atmosphere. There was a family of six who had alcoholic drinks included in their price and they kindly allowed me to get my alcohol on their tab. I was very pleased about this and took them up on their offer. I pretty much drank from the afternoon to the evening every day, after all I was on holiday.

On my second to last day of the holiday I met up with my chef and he asked me for some money, I did not have much money on me at the time so I told him I would give him what I had left over the following night. Besides I hated men asking me for money, but a part of me felt sorry for him because his wages were so menial. So on my last night, I went down to the beach to meet him, however he was not there, I waited ages, walking up and down the beach looking for him. He did not turn up, I was extremely upset, I had money for him, a box of cigarettes and I wanted to take his address and write to him, but it was not to be. In desperation I even left my address with one of my holiday friends I had made and asked her to give it to him if she saw him, I never did hear from him.

My counselling sessions were progressing well and I felt I was becoming stronger and more aware of my issues and learned behaviour. Mary was very subtle in her suggestions, sometimes so subtle I did not actually get what she was trying to say. I would tell her about what went on for me in the preceding week. I discussed my escapades out clubbing and how much I really enjoyed myself. Mary asked me if I would enjoy it so much if I did not drink, I was convinced that I would even though I had never tried it. I just knew that clubbing was now a big part of my life; I had a lot of catching up to do!

Mary and I would periodically discuss Naomi's progress and we felt she was doing ok. However, I was finding it difficult to cope with Adrian, he seemed to be so restless and needed constant attention, Mary suggested that I think about sending him to a playgroup, she said that he was just a very intelligent child that needed stimulating. I looked into this and managed to get his name on a waiting list at a playgroup in Claude Road not far from where we lived. Eventually a space came for him and I was elated, it meant he would get to mix with kids his own age and I would get a little break.

One of the counselling sessions was about how I portrayed myself, especially with the clothes I wore and how I danced when I was out. Mary asked me if I would dance provocatively and I said yes I did, that's how I danced, and I liked to express myself. Deep down I realised that dancing that way got me loads of dances with the guys, and I was certainly enjoying the attention I was getting. Because I was very sexual in my behaviour especially when out clubbing the conversation led to the topic of sexual abuse, I asked her, "Do you think my stepdad sexually abused me?" Mary responded, "If he did you would remember." I was a little confused and seeing as I had no recollection apart from that one occasion where I told my mum about the so-called family friend I just went on my merry way. Nevertheless I found it extremely difficult to deal with my daughter's abuse, if ever I told anyone about it, I would just start crying, it was just so painful for me to know that my daughter had been molested.

As much as I enjoyed my time when the kids were not around I still missed them, I would fill my time by going to aerobics or circuit training and clubbing. Clubbing and training were now a big part of my life and I would go out Friday and Saturday night. The Players Club had recently opened up in East Ham and it started off just being a wine bar, Georgia, Sandy, Marcia and I, all ex witnesses, would go there every Friday for a drink. I met Anna at aerobics and we became good friends, she also started to join us. After a few weeks word got around and Players suddenly took off as the club to be at on a Friday night in the East End of London. The license on the club meant that it would close at 1.00am in the morning.

My girls and I were all regulars at Players and it was a storm! Corks had been our regular joint up until now and I convinced Gill, Natalie and their crew to also come down to Players. I would often be the one to organise our nights out to

Players and try and get everyone together. There were times when there was a crowd of about 15 girls from North, South and East London. It was great fun, we would dance the night away and the majority of us were quite drunk by the end of the night. At about 12.45 the DJ would play soca and we would dance our hearts out, even when the lights came on we were still dancing. The 1.00am finish was far too early.

There were many regular faces there and some of the eye candy was just to die for. We met a guy named Martin and he invited us back to his place, he had a lovely home in Wanstead and he was very gentlemanly. He became very good friends with Anna and I. He would treat us to copious amounts of brandy and champagne; he was quite well off and was very well known. As time went on the relationship between the three of us became quite strange, which I did not realise until it was brought to my attention at my counselling session by Mary. It seemed like he played Anna and I against each other. I could not understand this as it was clear to me that he had the hots for Anna. However, I enjoyed their company and during the day they would sometimes come over, drink, talk and just hang out.

He had a birthday party not long after we met and he invited all the girls. In true form we turned up early ready for a good time. We started drinking early and before the party really kicked off I was out of it. I was taken upstairs to his bedroom and Anna stayed with me to make sure I was ok. I felt sick and my head was spinning. Anna and Natalie tried to take me outside in the hope that the fresh air would help sober me up a little. But they could not manage my dead weight. So I had to sit it out, until the point came when I needed to throw up and they managed to get a bucket just in time. Once I threw up

I passed out and was out for at least two hours. When I came to, Anna was still there, she had kept an eye on me all that time. I managed to get up tidied myself, put on some lipstick and went downstairs to re-join the party. I acted as if nothing had happened and was gutted that I missed most of the party.

Adrian's pre-school nursery place had come up at Central Park and I was pleased that he was getting older. I decided to take the afternoon slot and keep him on at playgroup in the morning. It was a little stressful; I would drop him off to playgroup drive to the leisure centre for my aerobics class, go home, shower, cook his lunch, then pick him up, feed him quickly and drop him off to nursery. It was a matter of every second counts and sometimes Georgia would come back to mine and shower have her lunch and go to work, I sometimes ended up being late because of this which I found quite annoying.

Naomi was having swimming lessons; she enjoyed it and was doing very well. As Adrian got a little older I decided to book him lessons also. I felt it was important for them to be able to swim, I loved swimming myself and it was good to see my children having fun in the water. I was so impressed with them when we went to Tunisia as they were brave enough to go into the sea when we went on a boat ride. The water was deep but they were given a dinghy, I was not as brave as them. Adrian was a tough student; he was very stubborn and just wanted to do his own thing. He would not listen and follow instructions, his instructor found it hard to teach him and no matter how much I talked to him to behave and follow instructions it seemed to fall on hard ears. In the end I decided to stop his lessons, it was a waste of time and money. Oh he was such hard work.

Adrian was very upset over the split and years later he still found it difficult to accept. He was very hyper and would often cry over the fact that his dad no longer lived with us. I would moan about him and someone said to me, "But the apple does not fall far from the tree." Those words stung, and I thought that I really needed to make some changes here. I tried to spend more quality time with the children at the same time trying to change my behaviour around them. I was always doing something, I found it hard to sit with myself, housework was always a priority, Mary often told me to let the housework go sometimes, but I found it difficult to let go. She also gave me lots of tips on how to be a better parent for my children. She gave me alternatives to smacking which I liked because I did not like the idea of hitting my children, especially when I thought about the way I was brought up. I really valued how much I learned from Mary regarding raising my children.

One of my main worries was that my children would be deeply scarred by the breakup of my marriage; I did not want them to turn out like me, constantly depressed and lacking self esteem. Mary assured me that this would not happen as their childhood was very different from mine. Mary pointed out the fact that the emotional abuse that I suffered at the hands of my step-father was a main reason for my depression and the way I turned out, and my kids had not been treated badly by a step parent. A few years passed and I was still having counselling, still clubbing and learning about myself and how to make better choices in my life, well some of the time anyway. By this time,

Mary and I decided it would be good for Adrian to have some counselling for himself to help him deal with the break up.

Chapter 27

Looking for Love

Whenever I went clubbing I would always get drunk. Some of the girls would meet up at my house first and we would have a drink or two to get in the mood for the night ahead. If we went to Corks, we would get the train down and take a cab back, that way we could all drink. On the tube we were 'women behaving badly,' but we did not care. By the end of the night, there were occasions when I would lose money and did not have enough to chip in my part of the cab money, it baffled me how I managed to lose money, I was always very careful; so I thought.

I met my fair share of guys whilst out clubbing, Burton I met at Corks; he was over six foot tall and had a very deep voice, it turned me on. He was single and took me on a couple of dates, I spent the weekend at his and he also spent it at mine. I think he wanted our relationship to flourish, however I stressed to him that I was not looking for anything serious I just wanted to have some fun. Burton went with the flow and did not put any pressure on me; he was a real cool guy, but such a sloppy kisser.

There was a bit of an overlap when I started seeing Henry a guy I met at Caesars' night club in South London; he had a partner, although they were not married. We had loads of deep conversations and that was the main part of our relationship, he was about 10 years older than I was. He lived in South London and we did not really see each other often, albeit we spoke on the phone every day. Each day I eagerly awaited his call; I lived for his phone calls. We only slept together twice in an empty looking flat which he must have used to entertain his bits on the side. Everything seemed so very controlled with him.

As my counselling progressed I grew mentally stronger and found that I was no longer intrigued by this guy and put an end to the phone calls. Besides I also got a call from his girlfriend telling me to stay well clear. I felt bad that I had been messing around with her man. I then met Oscar. The night we met, we danced all night long without coming up for air. He took my number and that was the beginning of our affair. He told me he was married on our first phone conversation, I told him I was not interested and he insisted that we could be friends, so I agreed. I found it difficult, we clicked and I enjoyed our conversations. Before long we ended up sleeping together. I felt terribly guilty, and would often communicate this to him, he assured me that I had nothing to be guilty about because I was not the one that was married. But I could not help feeling sorry for his wife. One minute I called it off and the next it was back on again. I did not want to be the other woman, and a part of me wished that he would leave his wife, although he always stressed that was never going to be an option.

Mary knew about this affair, I could tell her everything. She tried to get me to see that it was harmful for me to be in this relationship. There were times that I would forget (on purpose) to turn my phone off whilst in session and he would ring. I could see the annoyance on Mary's face she did not like the way he was influencing my life and even to the point of intruding into my counselling sessions. The relationship was not healthy, but I did not care, I was hooked and happy to have snippets of this man's time even though it was not really quality time. He called me every day apart from weekends and I was satisfied with that.

I finally came to my senses and decided to end it with Oscar, I started to feel that he was trying to control my life and he had no right to do so, especially as he would not leave his wife for me. Needless to say he was not happy with my decision, but I knew it was for the best. We remained friends for a good few years.

I became very frustrated that I could not meet anyone who was single and willing to have a relationship; I started to think that all men were dogs. Then I met Jerome he was absolutely gorgeous, tall with wavy black hair he was mixed race although predominantly black. We passed each other in Corks stopped and started talking; there was definitely an instant attraction. I was wearing what I called my fuck off dress, aqua blue mini and skin tight. Even though I was a size 16 I was still training regularly and very toned. He told me to come and look for him later for a dance.

I enjoyed the night although I did not go looking for him, I thought that he should come looking for me, he was the guy and men were meant to do the chasing. At the end of the evening we saw each other again, and he asked me why I did not come and look for him, I said, "The same way I can come and look for you, you can come and look for me, besides you're the man aren't you?" Anyway we started talking and before I knew it he ended up coming back in the cab with us. He came back to my house and I told him that I do not sleep with guys on the first night. To my surprise he was not expecting to get into my knickers, he just wanted a cuddle and I thought this was really sweet. We talked and he teased me and called me a 'removal artist' because I took off my blond curly wig and took out my hazel contact lenses. He wondered if I was going to take fillets out of my bra, but mine were real.

I met up with Jerome regularly, I was quite keen to see him and would always be the one to do the calling, but I did not mind. I would drive down to Elephant and Castle to see him. We would go for drinks and he taught me how to play pool, we had fun together. Even though we slept together, he never called it a relationship so I would not be as intimate with him as he wanted me to be. He often complained that I would just turn my back on him after we had sex rather than cuddle up afterwards.

I became very fond of Jerome however, there came a point when things started to change between us, he would sometimes say some cutting remarks in jest, however, I was sensitive and found them very hurtful. I would end up being a bit of a bitch towards him at times, and our fun evenings started to turn sour. I decided that this was not for me, I hated the way I started to feel around him, very inadequate and fearful so I stopped seeing him even though I really liked him.

I met a guy at Visions in Dalston; he gave my friends and me a lift home and walked me to the door leaving his friend in the car. He invited himself in and we started to have a bit of a kiss. I had to stop him from going any further because at that time I was prescribed Xenicol weight loss tablets, which caused me to pass fat through my stools, so every time I passed wind, my panties were 'for my eyes only' therefore I sent him on his merry way. However before leaving he said, "You're very pretty but you would look much better if you were to lose some weight." 'HOW VERY DARE HE?' I thought. Instead I said, "Well what are you doing with me if you think I'm too fat, and why don't you go and look for a slim girl?" I was actually deeply offended and quite upset; anyway he was a skinny bastard whose name I cannot even remember!

Another young man I met at Visions; was very young, about 21 but he was so keen. This boosted my ego and I met up with him once and he visited me at my home. He blatantly just came out and requested "Suck my dick," now he was a big lad if you know what I mean, besides I was somewhat disgusted and told him "Hell no, I am not some little gal from the street, besides it is too big and I don't fancy choking on it!" Needless to say that was the end of that.

I even had a couple of one night stands, this was not my intention, I just did not realise that these guys were only interested in one thing. Boy was I naive. I remember a couple of occasions at Corks when I would dance with guys behaving like a proper little tart flinging myself up on them, kissing them and allowing them to rub my breasts on the dance floor, I was like a wild cat on heat. Where did my Christian upbringing go?

Chapter 28

The Entertainer

I filled some of my time with going to amateur dramatic classes at the new Stratford Circus. My first tutor was a guy named Derek, I loved the way he taught and I thoroughly enjoyed my classes. I met some really interesting people on those courses Raymond being one of them, a tall handsome English born Guyanese man, we had an instant connection. We would joke around together something chronic, it was such fun and I felt free and happy doing something that I enjoyed with people that understood me. We put on performances at the end of each course and were allowed to invite friends and family. I loved taking part in the performance, yep you got it, and I liked being the centre of attention! Derek was very pleased with the work I produced, and always encouraged me to go further and get an agent.

I was always the life and soul of the party, constantly making people laugh, and forever smiling. My way of hiding what was going on inside and it worked a treat. My friends would often comment that I should have been a comedian. I heard it so many times that I started to think about it and casually started writing stuff down. If I made people laugh I would write down what I said and before long I had quite a lot of material under my belt. Marcia then introduced me to a promoter, I met with him and showed him my material, he said it was pretty funny and advised me to just go along to the

Bullion Room Theatre in Hackney where they were having the All Stars Stand Up Comedy competition. I thought he was having a laugh; excuse the pun; however he said it was not to win but just to start getting some experience. I took his advice:

Marcia and Raymond came with me to offer moral support and I do not know what I would have done without them. It was on a sunny Sunday afternoon, everything seemed so bright yet I was as nervous as hell. I could not believe I was putting myself through this. I needed to practise when I arrived even though I had been practising in the days preceding. I was pacing up and down unable to settle for one minute. I had so many thoughts of turning around and going home, the nerves were that bad. I brought along some vodka just to settle my nerves, thank God for that. I saw some of the acts and was not impressed with a few, although others were pretty good. Some of the comedians sounded as if they had some serious issues going on and were having difficulty delivering their material in a funny way, I found it quite distressing to hear.

Finally my time came to go on and I wanted the ground to open up and swallow me, however, I had come this far, so I had to go through with it and I did. Once I got up on the stage it did not seem half as bad, I rushed through my routine, not giving my audience enough time to laugh. Nevertheless, they laughed, they found me funny, they weren't hysterical but they laughed. I came off the stage feeling pretty chuffed with myself as the applause rang loudly in my ears. I liked the feeling, I liked the attention. Marcia and Raymond gave me feedback and said I was good considering it was my first time. That was the beginning of my Stand up Comedy.

Between 2002 and 2004 I did gigs at different clubs and bars in London including the Rawspot Juggling Comedy Show, Kennedy's Comedy Show, Vocals Talent Show and Angie Lemar's Comedy Store to name a few. Audiences seemed to love me, well they laughed and at times hysterically, performing gave me a buzz second to none.

Chapter 29

Turning Thirty – 1998 - 2001

I was approaching 30 and I started to panic, I felt that my life was passing me by and I had not achieved anything apart from having two lovely children. I did not want to be 30 because to me it meant that it was time for me to be grown up and become serious, but I did not feel ready for that. I was just starting out, feeling quite rebellious, I had even started smoking, It started off with a cigarette here and a cigarette there, then It crept up to a few when I went out and before I knew it I was smoking at least 10 a day. I hid this fact from the children, I did not want to smoke around them and I did not want them to know either because I did not want them influenced by my smoking. I would often hang out of my bedroom window with my cigarettes and welcomed the times when they were at their dad which meant I could smoke freely.

I decided to have a party for my birthday. After all those years of not celebrating birthdays due to 'the religion' I felt I deserved a good old party. I invited loads of people, all my girls, some of the guys from training and guys I had met from clubbing. I told people that they could bring friends if they wished and asked them all to bring a bottle. I went shopping for an outfit with Anna, Marcia and Julia – Julia I met through Anna – down Font Hill Road. It was dire, I could not find an outfit I liked that would fit, all the outfits I liked I was too fat for, it was so disheartening. My stomach was huge! 'Why couldn't I be slim and slender like the rest of my friends?' I was bemused. Finally I managed to find a long red dress with a long split up the side and decided it would have to do, even though not much cleavage was on show; I liked showing my cleavage, 'If you got it, flaunt it' was my motto!

I received a lot of help from my friends; Anna and Julia spent most of the day helping me prepare the salads cook the chicken and rice. Georgia and Sandy made curry goat, Marcia did the coleslaw. Everyone was so helpful and very excited about the party. Anna's boyfriend and his brother played the music for the party.

The day flew by and before long it was time to get ready for the party. I started drinking as soon as it was feasibly possible, around mid- afternoon! The party did not take long to kick off, after all I was the host and I knew how to party. The party was absolutely brilliant; there were loads to drink, more than enough food, a good turnout of people and the music was great. I enjoyed being the centre of attention and dancing with whomever I chose to as it was my birthday, I certainly made sure I got around. The party ended at 9.00am the following morning, everyone was raving about it. I subsequently had three more birthday parties although each one was not as good as the previous.

Chapter 30

Drunken Nights

Natalie had a get together for her birthday one year and she lived in South London. I was the only one who knew where she lived out of those from the East that was to attend. However prior to us going down there, Anna, Julia, Martin and I met up late afternoon and drank Bacardi 151 which Martin had purchased from the States. The drink was 151% proof, thus the name Bacardi 151. Martin had to go off and do something so he left the drink with us and told us to take time with it, due to its strength. Well it seemed like Anna and I had one too many of the drink and we ended up getting totally and utterly out of it. We started jumping around out in my front garden where Anna bruised her leg. We were making too much noise so went back inside and started jumping on my bed and behaving very silly. I threw up in my bathroom and poor Julia cleaned it up for me, how very sweet of her. We managed somehow to compose ourselves, get showered and ready for Natalie's get together.

Martin and his friend turned up to drive us all down to South London. When they arrived they could not believe how much of the drink had gone. They also could not believe the state we were in; we thought we were putting on a good show of being sober. Martin said there was no way that we could go to Natalie's in that state. We managed to convince him that we were ok and that I would be able to direct them to her house.

Do not ask me how I did that, but I did considering I had been to Natalie's new place only once before.

When we arrived, everyone looked at us in shock, I was told. I just sat on the sofa, asking for water every five minutes. I could not converse with anyone and apparently the way I was seated was very un-lady like. Yet I believed I was doing a good job of being sober.

I enjoyed getting drunk when I went out, it made the night fun. There were times when I was broke so I would hide miniatures in my cleavage when going to clubs. My cleavage was big enough to hold more than one miniature or even a small water bottle; with alcohol inside, if I placed it strategically. I never got caught, obviously as security search our bags not our breasts! It made for a cheap night out without us having to worry about spending too much on alcohol.

On one occasion at Players a random man came up to me admiring my boobs, he told me, "Your boobs look lovely, can I feel them?" A Little shocked but chuffed I said, "Yes, but you will have to pay me for the privilege." "How much?" he asked. "£20," I replied. He took out his £20 note and proceeded to put it in between my cleavage, not letting it go he then cupped his hand over my right breast. By now I started to feel a little uncomfortable and instantly said, "OK that's enough." He was still holding onto the note and I quickly snatched it out of his hands, smiled sweetly and said "Thank you". Off I went with a wiggle of my hips towards the ladies. I was so excited about being £20 better off for the night; I used it to treat some of the girls and Martin to drinks.

For one of my birthdays, the girls and I celebrated the Friday night at Players, as it was my birthday people were buying me drinks, and I never said no; why would I? Anthony was there for some reason and I was excited to see him because he still wanted me back and I was beginning to think that I was not going to find anyone else anyway. I had mentioned to some of the girls that I still had some feelings for him, as a lot of time had passed and the anger that we both had seemed to have subsided.

I was enjoying the night and then all of a sudden I spotted Sandy going over to Anthony and dancing up behind him, whining herself on him. I grew up with Sandy so I don't know what the... I saw red I was livid! 'What the hell did she think she was doing?' I thought. I could not control myself and I went up to her grabbed her by the neck and started shouting at her at the top of my voice, she looked petrified and started apologising. I shouted some more and told her to stay away from him. I had created such a scene and friends were trying to get me off her and calm me down. They managed to tear me away from Sandy, but I was still not calm. I was shouting and cussing and throwing glasses on the floor in rage. In the end they decided to take me home so I could sleep it off. Even I didn't know I had it in me to behave that way. What would my mother think?

Another birthday at Players and then onto Visions, I drank so much that my friends had to carry me out of the place and take me home. They got me to the front door where I was giggling and they were trying to get the key out of my bag, I was making it difficult for them in my drunken stupor. I had to be carried up to my bed at my grandmothers' house, where my kids were sleeping quietly. I passed out by the time my head hit the pillow.

There came a point when I started to get sick of this behaviour, all I wanted was to find a decent boyfriend, I did not like being on my own. I was such a socialite and always appeared to be enjoying myself whilst out with the girls. However when at home alone, it was awful, the silence was deafening, the hangovers were awful. I even had alcohol poisoning a couple of times causing my eyes to become as red as a beetroot and pains in my back due to liver infection. Surely there was more to life than this.

Chapter 31

Getting Serious

I felt like I was going downhill, I was only working one day a week again at Morgan Stanley, partying hard and thinking that I would not be able to get a job paying more than £20,000. I felt like I needed to be working but not having the courage to go for it. Martin encouraged me and told me in no uncertain terms that I could easily get a job paying more than that, and proceeded to ask me to get him a pair of scissors. Perplexed I brought him the scissors and he then started to cut the sleeve of his jacket, I was gobsmacked and asked him what he was doing. His response was that, because he worked money was really no object to him; he could simply go out and buy another jacket. Weird as it was, his performance spurred me into action; I started looking for work.

I was fortunate enough to land a job at my favourite place Morgan Stanley, it was ideal for me, 10.00-2.00 every day, paying £12 per hour. I had time to take the kids to school and also pick them up. My life started to get better, the money gave me more freedom to do the things I wanted and I was now able to keep my brain stimulated. The job was perfect with regard to the children however it was in the least challenging. I was working for a small team in the Investment Management department consisting of two Dutch investment bankers and their analyst. I enjoyed working for them and often asked for more responsibilities, albeit they did not have much more work to give me. I was quite bored and would spend a lot of my time on the phone or going for cigarette breaks. I didn't complain as it was an easy life really.

I took a fancy to one of my bosses, and I let him know about it when we had our department summer drinks. Drinking loads and snacking on canapés I was having a lovely time. I even wanted to impress him by smoking one of the cigars he and another colleague were smoking. I thought I was being cool. He did not take me up on my advances and told me that he did not want to hurt me because it looked like I was looking for something serious. I was a little hurt, but glad that he respected me enough to be honest. This did not stop us flirting on a daily basis though. That's how I got through my boring days of unchallenging work.

My first works Christmas party was something I fervently looked forward to. I had made friends with Eleanor who worked in another area of Investment Management and hoped that I would be sitting next to her at the party. However, I was sat amongst absolute strangers. I could not bear it, I found it so difficult to converse with people and I just wanted to slide under the table. After a few drinks however, I felt a lot more comfortable talking to those on my table although I still could not wait for the disco to start. Once that music started I was on my way drinking, dancing and enjoying myself.

Some time went by and I managed to tear myself away from the dance floor to go to the ladies. On my way back an Asian guy who worked for our department in IT approached me, his name was Suresh, he asked me a few questions about myself and I politely answered and went back to the party. When it was time to go home, Suresh was suddenly right by my side asking me if he could share a taxi home as he lived in Gallions Reach which was not too far from where I lived. I did not mind and saving money on the fare was appealing enough. We both got into the same taxi and before I could breathe Suresh was kissing me (I did not see that coming); we were kissing very passionately in the taxi all the way to my home. The taxi man seemed to have arrived at my house in half the time, he probably thought we were going to have sex in the back of his taxi and was having none of that slackness. I did not anticipate Suresh getting out of the taxi at my house, but he did. Clothes were strewn everywhere all over the hallway and up the stairs. We ended up in bed having mad passionate sex. No sooner as the deed was over Suresh was gone leaving me to sleep off my alcohol and whatever else...

The following morning at work I had a terrible hangover and a big grin on my face. Once at work, my first priority was to have a big old fry up for breakfast to help get me through the day. I emailed Suresh just wishing him a merry Christmas. I did not get a reply! This made me feel a bit used, but I pushed that feeling to the back of my mind because at least I enjoyed myself.

This made me really think about how I behaved with men and discussed it with Mary and as I continued to develop and grow I was starting to change my behaviour with men, I made a concerted effort to not sleep with anyone unless I was in a relationship with them. It was a little challenging but I succeeded.

Chapter 32

Visit to Daddy - 2002

Due to my counselling I realised that some of my issues were due to the fact that my biological father was not around for me and I thought it would be good for me to start building up that relationship. I needed a break, so Christmas 2002 I thought it would be nice to get away and arranged a visit to New York to see my dad; it had been years since my last visit.

He was keen to have me and I was excited to be going. Unfortunately I could not afford to bring the children so I asked their dad if he would have them whilst I went away. He agreed and as I packed their clothes, following advice from my counsellor, I put little notes in their clothes saying things like 'I will miss you,' 'I love you very much,' 'be good now' and 'enjoy yourself.' I was sad to leave them for two weeks, but I knew they would be fine with their dad.

When I arrived in New York, dad picked me up from JFK Airport in his beaming champagne coloured Lexus, although he did not drive it, his friend did. Apparently he only drove it in the local neighbourhood. It was good to see him, he had not aged at all from the last time I saw him when he came over to England in 1996. The drive to his house was about 30 minutes, which was pleasant enough even though it was along the highway.

His house was large; the building was split into four apartments with a basement. I was impressed, however my dad had rented out all the apartments to help pay the mortgage and he lived in the basement. As I walked into the basement area of the house, it was dark and towards the right was a bar, then in the centre of the main room were a couple of tables with dominoes scattered across them. There was a door which led into a bedroom with a double bed, the room was rather small. Near the end of the main room toward the right was a large kitchen and next door to that was a tiny bathroom and at the end of the apartment was a room full of furniture and a bed where my dad's cousins were staying. 'Where was I going to sleep?' I wondered.

To my horror I had to share a bed with my dad, how inappropriate was that? I felt I could not really say anything, as I did not want to seem ungrateful. It was an awful experience sharing a bed with my dad whom I had not grown up with. We had separate covers but I still felt uneasy. I found it difficult to relax and could not sleep properly; I was scared in case our bodies accidentally touched. Was I mad?

I did not really enjoy my holiday as it was not what I had expected, my dad had the local guys around most evenings drinking, making lots of noise whilst playing dominoes, and literally banging the tables in the customary way that West Indians do. I hated them being there because they would all eye me up whenever I was around; they were old perverts as far as I was concerned. My dad actually worked over the Christmas season even on Christmas day itself. That was very disconcerting, I flew all the way over from England to spend Christmas with my dad and he works on Christmas day. He came back from work in time for dinner which his cousins had prepared with some assistance from me.

The dinner table looked stupendous they cooked turkey, gammon, rice and peas, Brussels sprouts, macaroni cheese, coleslaw, homemade carrot juice, Guinness punch, sorrel and more. It was a feast and I could not wait to tuck in. We all sat around the dinner table and my dad gave thanks to the Lord and we started to eat passing dishes around the table. The food was good and I enjoyed every bit of it, although I felt that the atmosphere around the table was a little strained. I was delighted and relieved that my sister Sandra had come over for dinner as we always got on really well and it was good to see her after so many years. She had a little girl now, Samaria she called her and she was adorable.

My days were long and boring until one day my cousin took me out to a shopping outlet in New Jersey, we were accompanied by her boyfriend, and two of his friends. The car journey was long and I was in the back with my cousin who we called Dungee (God knows where that name came from), Rick and Gordon. The atmosphere was a little strained, it just seemed so intense. We made polite conversation, and they were thrilled to have an English girl in the car, as the Americans just love our accents.

Don't ask me how this happened but Gordon and I were instantly attracted to each other despite the fact that he did have a girlfriend whom he lived with. We held hands in the shopping centre and talked and behaved as if we were a couple. From then on he called me every day and came to visit at my dad's house where we would go for walks even in the snow, or just sit in the car and talk. He always referred to me as being sweet and at the end of each conversation he would say "Stay as sweet as you are." I was in love!

One day my father approached me and told me that he didn't like the fact that I was seeing this guy and spending so much time with him. I was outraged, 'How fucking dare he tell me that?' I thought. He was the one who hardly took any time off work to spend with me, he was the one who didn't even think about where I would sleep so had me sharing his bed, how wrong was that? He was the one that only had time for his stupid Haitian girlfriend who was pregnant with his child and she was only one year older than me. I broke down and cried and cried and cried. My dad did not know what to do or even say, although he did say, "How do you expect me to feel with you crying like that?" There he went again, 'It's all about him' I thought, this man will never be the father I want or indeed deserve, and I believe that was why I was crying. Those tears spoke volumes, they helped me heal somewhat.

I carried on seeing Gordon despite my dad and we talked about our future, he said he would come to see me in England. He seemed to be genuine and also seemed as if he was agonizing over his situation and what he was going to do about it. The day before I was due to leave we were in the car having a kiss and a cuddle, I got caught up in the moment and suggested we go in the back, he was such a gentleman and said "No, because I want to do right by you." I felt ashamed that I was so quick to let him in. He was so respectful, gentle and sweet, he had even taken me out to a dance, where my sister Connie accompanied us and he paid for her also. We gave each other photographs of ourselves and exchanged telephone numbers. I was very sad to leave him behind and cried quietly into my pillow that night.

I was more than happy to be home; the main reason being was that I missed my children. Marcia picked me up from the airport and I was at her house when Anthony dropped the kids off. I was outside when they saw me from afar and they ran up to me and straight into my arms, shouting out "Mummy!" I was over the moon to see them and them me. Back home, I told them bits of information about my trip and gave them their presents and clothes that I had bought for them.

I had put the pictures of Gordon up in my bedroom and called him to let him know I had arrived safely. I texted him every other day too, and he would respond although not immediately. I came to the realisation that I was the one doing all the calling or initiating the texting. This made me stop and think and decided to not call or text just to see how long it would be before he would get in touch. I waited two weeks before he called and by that time it was too late...

Chapter 33

Swept Off My Feet - 2003

I was at Illusions, a club in South London with Natalie and her friend Jackie, about a week or so after New Years. I was having a mediocre time and was not drunk as I had calmed down on my drinking, besides I was driving, not that it ever stopped me drinking in the past. It was a little dead, not much of a vibe and I could not see much talent in the room, I always did a scan. Suddenly I spotted someone; he was standing with his back towards the bar, in a very relaxed fashion, with his elbows on the bar. He had dreadlocks, was slim about 5'10," his complexion was a honey brown, a little lighter than myself, his eyes looked dreamy and our eyes locked for about three seconds. I immediately thought to myself, "Wow, he is gorgeous". I turned around to tell Natalie and by the time I turned back around, he was gone. I did not go looking for him, stand nearby him or anything like that, even though I wanted to. Nevertheless I started to become uneasy thinking, 'Where the hell is he?'

Finally, there he was in front of me and asking me for a dance, his hand held out in a polite fashion, before he could finish asking me I was already in his arms. He introduced himself as Leonard, and we started to dance to the slow tones of the reggae music. He seemed a little intoxicated but nothing to be concerned about. We were practically inseparable as we danced and talked together. He was born in Jamaica and was in

England for the first time on a holiday, he had been here for only two weeks. He talked about working for his family business in Jamaica and how he used to be a dental technician and wanted to pursue that career here in England. I was quite impressed with how educated and successful he appeared to be. He also mentioned that he would be applying to the home office to extend his holiday visa for six months. He had spent the weekend with his cousin Tommy in Thornton Heath, but was actually staying with his cousin Dina in Ilford. It was a bit of a coincidence because I lived only two or three miles from Ilford and was staying with Natalie in Croydon.

We were locked in each other's' arms, mainly talking and finding out about each other, he was very direct and asked me what I was looking for and by this time in my life I had had enough so I told him plainly in no uncertain terms that I was looking for a serious relationship. He said he could offer that, which I took on the chin and quietly thought to myself, quite cynically, 'We shall see, only time will tell.' The night was coming to an end and Natalie and Jackie were ready to go home, I informed him of this, however, he did not want to let me go, I was so enjoying myself and was chuffed at how keen he was and we exchanged numbers. As I walked towards the car I felt light on my feet, a bit of a miracle when you consider how heavy I was.

I tried to stay cool but was becoming agitated when I had not heard from him on the Monday. I thought to myself, 'If he does not call by Wednesday, then that's it.' I heard from him by the Tuesday when he asked me out for a drink that same evening. Tuesday's were handy for me because the children spent that time as well as Thursday's with their dad. Leonard was dropped off to my house by his cousin in law Linford, and when he saw me he seemed to be in awe and told me how much nicer I looked in the day time. We then proceeded in my car to Fox's a wine bar in Stratford. We talked intimately and he asked me if I would be his girlfriend. I nearly fell off my chair in complete shock, because that was the first time that someone had asked me right out, no beating around the bush, no playing with my head. For a split second I pondered because we did not really know each other, however, one thing I did know was that I was really attracted to him and so far he had been a gentleman. I found myself saying yes. Time seemed to go by so quickly and I had to be home by 9.30 for the children, so I offered to drop him off at the bus stop near Woodgrange Road on my way home. He did not want to get out of the car, it was as if he did not want to be parted from me and I thought he was so sweet, I believe that's when he fell in love with me.

After these five years of being single I thought to myself 'How simple was that!' I called him the following day and asked him if he wanted to come over to watch a film, he said yes and asked what he should bring, that went down well in my books, not wanting to arrive empty handed. I said he could bring a drink or popcorn and to come after 8.00pm once I had put the children to bed. He arrived at 8.30pm with some popcorn and a drink. Don't ask me what film we watched because we did not really watch it even though it was playing in the background. We just talked all evening, mainly about the future, he had great ambition and I loved that in him. He was such a gentleman, and in the middle of the conversation he asked "Can I kiss you?" I shyly responded with, "Yes". It was lovely, and the sparks were definitely there, very romantic. The time had drifted by effortlessly and before we knew it the early hours of the morning had loomed upon us. I said he could stay so we both ended up kipping on the sofa.

We woke up quite early, about 6.30am and we sat in the kitchen smoking, drinking coffee and talking. By the time the kids woke up I was petrified, because I had made a point of them never seeing men in my house unless they were just friends. I heard them coming down the stairs and I did not know what to say to them about this dread in my house, he told me to be up front and honest with them, and he was right, kids were not stupid anyway. They came into the kitchen still half asleep and looking bemused, I introduced them to Leonard and told them that they would be seeing more of him, because he was my boyfriend. They politely said hello and then I got them their breakfast and let them get ready for school, whilst I also got ready for work.

During the day Leonard texted me a beautiful text message and asked me what I wanted for dinner as he wanted to cook for me. 'He cooks too? This is just too good to be true,' I thought. He arrived that evening with ingredients and cooked a lovely fish dish. I could certainly get used to this. He stayed that night, I was on my monthly so nothing happened in that department, and I was glad in a way because even though it felt very right I still wanted to wait for as long as possible. This happened to be just over a week from meeting him – not very long at all.

It was passionate, to say the least, and once we started, we could not stop, his appetite in that department was definitely a healthy one. He certainly lived up to the stereotype of 'Jamaicans certainly know how to fuck good.' However, I needed to coach him in the art of lovemaking which he welcomed and could see and feel the difference. It was just magic. Two weeks from our initial meet we were in the kitchen talking as per usual and somehow we were on the subject of marriage and before I knew it, he took a flower out of the bunch that he had brought me days before and went down on one knee and asked "Would you do me the honour of being my wife?," handing me the rose at the same time. I was gobsmacked to say the least, my very first thought being, 'Please don't ask me to marry you,' which instantly switched to me portraying the largest grin on my face and saying, "Yes."

Even though he had already been staying over ever since that first night; he officially moved all his clothes and belongings in. I was excited to have my new man move in with me, although a little resentful about giving him wardrobe space. I also let him know that I would not allow him to smoke his weed in the house, which he said he would respect. I did not bank on falling in love with someone who smoked it, in fact I had a list of what I wanted and did not want in a man; that was definitely something I did not want so I battled with accepting it.

We spoke about setting the date for the wedding, I was thinking about a year's time at least, in order to get to know him better, organise the wedding, and time for him to go back to Jamaica and apply for a visa to marry. Leonard, however, had other plans; he did not want to have to go back to Jamaica and wanted us to marry before his visitors' visa ran out in June. Immediately alarm bells started ringing and this sewed doubts into my mind; I thought that maybe he just wanted to marry me to stay in the country. However, he convinced me that he would be with me whether I married him or not. This put me at ease and I agreed to marry him on May 17th 2003.

That being said, we had work to do, a wedding to organise in just four months! Where would I start? My colleague Sarah was also getting married a little later than myself, but she had been organising her wedding for a year now. She gave me tips and spread sheets and was a great help and to be honest I don't know what I would have done without her help and input. Luckily I had just received a sizeable sum of money from the property which my ex-husband and I owned; he bought out my share of the house. I used about half of the money to pay for the wedding.

Leonard was working as a trainee dry liner, and was bringing in a pretty decent wage for someone who had just arrived in the country; his cousin in law Linford had helped him get the job. We set off one Saturday afternoon down to Lakeside to buy the engagement ring. It was a beautiful diamond cluster with a couple of diamonds going down both sides of the arm of the ring. We bought it from Beaver Brooks and we decided to buy our wedding rings at the same time, 18 carat white and yellow gold identical wedding bands. The service at Beaver Brooks was second to none, coffee and our very own personal assistant helping us to choose our rings, plus free aftercare service. Leonard did not have enough cash on him to purchase my engagement ring, so we decided to pay for it on my credit card and he would reimburse me. I was determined to have a ring at a decent price considering the price paid for my first ring by my first husband. This time round the ring was placed on my finger immediately by my fiancé. I was over the moon!

I had to meet the rest of his family and him mine. I was very nervous especially when it came to meeting his aunty who was known as his English mum. However, there was no need to be nervous as she was as warm and pleasant as could be and I liked her spirit. She even told me that if Leonard was to mess around, I must let her know and she would deal with him even though he was her nephew, in her eyes women had to stick together. This gave me so much reassurance. I had already met Tommy his cousin but went to meet his wife Shelly and their family, she talked a lot. I also met his cousin Dina, who was sweet and softly spoken. All in all, I liked his family, they were warm and friendly.

Organising the wedding was hectic, so much to do and so little time. Leonard only wanted a small family wedding, however, I wanted a big one and we ended up inviting 160 guests. I don't do things by halves, besides I wanted to show my new man off. My friends were really excited and happy for me and most offered their help and services. Nicola whom I had known for about seven years and was also an ex witness when I met her, offered to make my wedding dress for me and as her gift to me, she did not charge. My friend Joy's sister offered to do my flowers at cost price only. Pete, who was a chef at Morgan Stanley offered to do my catering and also did not charge me as much as he should have. Shelly's sister made the wedding cake and even catered for the fact that Leonard was a Vegan, making him his very own cake. My brother Shane paid for our limo as well as giving me away. I was proud to be on his arm, as he was such a kind and loving brother. Jay took my photos again and as per usual the photos were brilliant and he was kind enough to pay for them too. I was very grateful to everyone who contributed because the wedding turned out spectacularly.

It was hard to believe that the whole wedding only cost in the region of £9,000, because it looked like it cost at least £20,000. The day was a complete and utter panic; you see the wedding was booked for 12pm at Newham Registry Office and West Ham were playing football that day, so there was a lot of traffic in the area. My hairdresser arrived over an hour late, Naomi and Marley, Leonard's cousin, my flower girls were getting their hair done at the hairdressers just down the road and they were also running late. I had to ask my friend Shannon who lived round the corner to go and check on them and they had to literally run back to the house in order to get back on time. I also had to make sure that Adrian, who was my page boy, was dressed in his cream suit. It was mayhem and I thought that we were not going to make it. We managed to get to the registry office at about 12.15 and they were also running a little late, thank goodness.

I had to hide in another room so that Leonard could not see me until it was time for the ceremony. It was all so very romantic, I walked into the ceremony on my brothers' arms feeling quite nervous and excited. I could see all our guests and it was great to have them all present. I saw my groom, he looked very handsome and he wore a different suit to the one he had originally bought also wearing his waistcoat that matched the bodice of my dress, which Nicola had also made. The ceremony was beautiful, and we had chosen our own vows. Leonard became very emotional and cried pretty much throughout the ceremony, it was so sweet to see, and became the highlight of the wedding. I felt so happy and joyous. When the Clerk announced that we were now man and wife and said, "You may now kiss the bride," we kissed only to have Adrian moving in on us to see exactly what was going on; he became quite possessive of me for the rest of the day which I thought was really sweet.

We went onto West Ham Park to take photos, and the scenery was beautiful which was enhanced by the lovely weather. My brother snapped away and took some lovely photos. We had lots of time before the reception at 3.00pm, which was a bit of a wait for our guests. Back at the reception, we all talked and laughed whilst the room was being set up and waiting for the food to arrive, as there was an issue with the van overheating. However, the wait was worth it. When I walked into the hall it looked absolutely astonishing, Joy and her family had been in charge of making up the hall, and they did a fantastic job, I could not believe my eyes. From the flowers and rose petals, on the tables and the large pots by the side of the head table with extra-large flowers and greenery. I had made the favours myself with butterscotch sweets wrapped in gold contained in translucent plastic boxes. Everything just looked very classy and I was overjoyed, as my husband and I walked down toward the head table with everyone clapping and Natalie and Marcia, my bridesmaids throwing roses petals on the floor in front of us.

As I sat at the head table with my husband, children, bridesmaids and our respective mothers I felt so happy and contented albeit a little shy about eating knowing all eyes were on us. I really wanted to tuck into the food because Pete had done a fantastic job, the food was absolutely delicious. Our guests kept coming over to congratulate us and taking photos, which was lovely. To be honest I just wanted to get on with the party.

I had asked my bosses Steven and Michael to be our masters of ceremony, and they did a great job, as their sense of humour was very much appreciated by the guests. When it came to the speeches, I was so touched by what people said, from my brother Shane, to Leonard's aunty and Leonard himself, and me being me, I made sure I gave a speech which everyone found touching and extremely humorous. Cutting the cake was quite romantic as we both fed each other a piece of cake, although there was a point when we thought the cake was going to topple over. Our first dance was lovely and this is when I became quite emotional and shed a tear or two. Adrian came over to us after some time and politely asked Leonard if he could dance with me. It was such a lovely gesture and I felt really proud of him in the way he conducted himself, like a proper little gentleman.

The rest of the wedding was beautiful, with everyone enjoying themselves dancing and chatting, and I was certainly enjoying myself until there was trouble brewing. Carla, Troy's girlfriend's had attended and she did not get on with Jay my other brother. I had warned her to stay away from Jay at the wedding and she promised that she would, unfortunately, after a few drinks she forgot her promise and began to antagonise Jay, even to the point of spitting in his face. At this point Jay and Troy started to have words and nearly exchanged punches. They were all taken outside by my friends, Ronnie and Elaine. It all became quite heated with Carla and Paulette, Jay's girlfriend having a punch up. I was terribly upset and just wanted everyone to get on with each other and enjoy the wedding. I tried speaking to Carla and asked her why she had to start, and for her to consider what she had done, in essence, cause two brothers to fight at my wedding. Her very adamant response was, "Good!" I thought to myself, 'Good? Good?' I saw red and thought, 'What a bitch, she purposely wanted to cause trouble'. The red became so bright and before I could stop myself I gave her a hard slap across her face, well actually it was a bax! Elaine took me away from the whole debacle and back upstairs to the reception, by then I was shaking like a leaf disbelieving what I had just done on my own wedding day. I got myself a strong, long glass of vodka and downed it in one, which instantly made me feel much better. I then continued to enjoy my wedding.

Leonard and I stayed in a local hotel in Ilford that night, stopping off at home first to collect our things. The house was a complete mess and we did not have time to tidy up as we needed to check into our hotel. We ended up checking in late, but the hotel receptionist was kind and understanding. The room was modest and comfortable, and the bed looked inviting especially as I was quite exhausted. I was more than happy to just go to sleep and get some much needed rest, however, Leonard had other ideas and I felt obliged to make love to my husband on our wedding night.

The following morning we were up early – we had to get to Paddington to catch a train to Truro in Cornwall, where we would spend our honeymoon. Shane picked us up using my car and drove us to Paddington Station to get the 09.20 train. We had a wonderful time in Cornwall; we ate loads, drank even more and did what people do on honeymoons. We even had the hotel swimming pool to ourselves on several occasions. We played pool, with Leonard allowing me to win and me thinking that I won fairly and squarely; what a gentleman. We made time for excursions and walks along the beach and apart from it being rather cold we were very much in love and had a brilliant time taking photos at every opportunity.

Chapter 34

Struggles - 2004

Whilst on our honeymoon Leonard and I sent our marriage certificate to the Home Office, we had previously sent off the application before the cut-off date of May 14th 2003 when the law had changed regarding spouses visas, i.e. non British Nationals had to go back to their own country and apply for a visa before getting married. We played the waiting game and only two days before Leonard's visitors' visa had run out we received a letter stating that his application for a visa as my spouse was denied. Their cut-off date applied to the marriage date and not the application date. Alas, it was still too late as we had gotten married three days after the law had changed. He had to go back to Jamaica and apply for the visa there. I was devastated, my lovely new husband was expected to leave me and go back to Jamaica. I did not know how I would survive without him by my side.

We both felt sad and desperate so called upon the expert advice of a solicitor, citizen's advice bureaux and immigration themselves. The calls seemed endless, and we were becoming stressed. We made an appointment with a local solicitor and he advised us to appeal on the grounds of Human Rights. The wait seemed forever and in the meantime I had to start working full time; and lucky enough I applied for another job within my department which was full time, and was successful. It was for the sales team, very busy and fast paced. I welcomed the long awaited challenge and I enjoyed the wages at the end of the month. This job was permanent and becoming a permanent member of staff was ideal with all the benefits it entailed and at long last I really felt like I belonged at Morgan Stanley.

Leonard's work had dried up and he was not working as often and the jobs that did start coming through were for painting and decorating, which did not pay as well as dry lining. When he did not work, he was a house husband, cooking, cleaning and picking the kids up from school, and he also took on many DIY projects in the home. Not working affected his mood because he was not able to provide for us financially. He also had three kids of his own back in Jamaica, Kim, Brendon and Leonard Junior (LJ). They were lovely kids and I spoke to them when Leonard made his regular phone calls. Leonard spoke of Kim as being his heart beat and I could see why, she was so loving and understanding and it was obvious how much they missed each other, as she lived with Leonard and his family when he was in Jamaica.

Getting married again was tough on my children, especially Adrian. There was always a struggle between Leonard and Adrian both competing for my affections. I had to remind Leonard that he was the adult and should not antagonise Adrian which Leonard seemed to enjoy doing in a sadistic kind of way. They would often play fight, which was good for them to bond; however, Leonard would go too far and forget, maybe on purpose, that he had a lot more strength than Adrian, often leaving him in tears. I would often have to step in and warn Leonard to be gentler and not to upset my son. This sometimes led to us arguing, with Leonard saying that I spoilt Adrian and that he needed toughening up. But I was not about to let a step parent mistreat my children after what I went through as a child.

I had been suffering from extremely heavy and painful periods and was seeing a consultant at the local hospital; however, they could not seem to find out what was causing it. Fibroids were ruled out after a very long time of me using the Mirena coil. It was becoming tiresome for me and I felt at a loss. One day whilst in a local pub my period decided to show its face. I could feel the slight trickles and then I suddenly realised that they were no longer slight and told Leonard that we needed to leave immediately. As I got up, the chair had been soiled, I was so embarrassed and I could not believe this had happened so quickly. Luckily the pub was not packed, so we discreetly pushed the chair under the table and made a speedy exit. We got to the car, I placed my jacket on the seat and we drove home. Something did not feel right and when I got in the house I quickly ran into the bathroom and straight into the bath to shower. As soon as I got in the bath a whole load of stuff resembling liver covered in copious amounts of blood gushed out of my womb. Needless to say I don't know who was more frightened Leonard or me.

This had been going on for too long, I had suffered with bad periods ever since I started at age 13, but this saga had hit the jackpot. Something had to be done. Now that I had private healthcare through Morgan Stanley I decided to see a private GP who referred me to a gynaecologist in Harley Street. She organised for me to have an internal scan and they instantly discovered I had internal endometriosis. Within two weeks I was booked into a private hospital to have an endometrial ablation, where they burnt out the lining of my womb. I could not believe the efficiency of having private healthcare.

As time went on, my smoking increased, I could no longer hide it from my children. Leonard somehow managed to twist me around his finger into allowing him to smoke his weed in the house, at first I allowed him to smoke in the kitchen, but then it somehow managed to creep into the living room, even around my children. Was I losing my senses?

Chapter 35

Tragedy Strikes

Back in Jamaica, apparently there was a taxi driver in the area who was trying to molest the young girls in the neighbourhood and as Leonard was not around, Leonard's mother suggested that it would be better if Kim were to return to her own mother. Leonard still kept in contact with his daughter. It also came to my knowledge that there was an ex of Leonard's who was claiming that she had just given birth to a baby boy and Leonard was the father. At first Leonard did not want to believe her and thought that it was just her way of trying to get money from him now that he was in England. Leonard's mother reported back to Leonard that it was definitely his child as the baby looked just like him, his name was Travis. I was not happy to say the least, I married him knowing he had only three children, and was now taking on another step child. Regrettably nothing could be done about this even though it really did not sit well with me.

I was becoming tired of the repeated requests for money from the mothers of his children (three in total), it just seemed endless, so what little money he did earn a big chunk of it went to his children, which was fair albeit making it harder for us to make our life together. I suggested that he give them a set amount every month rather than giving it unexpectedly whenever they felt they needed it. This way I felt that we could budget in a more efficient way. However, there were still times when they wanted more, which enraged me. I felt that Leonard was guilty about not being there in person for his children so he felt obliged to give them as and when they asked. This would put untold pressure on our relationship and finances.

Kim became ill and of course, in Jamaica they have to pay for their medical bills. Leonard and I were on the phone with her very often to keep abreast of how she was doing. There were no real answers as to what was wrong with her, and when she worsened it took a very long time before her mother would take her to the hospital. She was in fact quite negligent and it appeared that Kim was suffering with severe headaches and her mother not really doing all she could to alleviate her child's suffering.

We sent money over to help pay for her bills, and Leonard was often in tears wishing that he could do more and missing her terribly. I even tried to see if Kim could receive treatment under my private healthcare insurance. Alas she was not living with us so she was not entitled to it. So we set about to file for her to come over to England for a visit in order to receive treatment here, this was also futile, immigration said that it was unlikely that she would return to Jamaica seeing as her dad had not. We felt at such a loss and helpless.

On February 11th 2004 Leonard and I were on our way to Windsor for Valentine weekend, we had booked a hotel and planned to have a romantic weekend together. It was early evening yet dark as we drove down the dual carriageway Leonard was on the phone with his mother from Jamaica, I was trying to focus on my driving so was not paying much attention to the phone call. Then his phone was ringing like crazy and texts messages were coming in thick and fast. I became a little concerned and wanted to know why everyone was calling him all of a sudden.

He then told me quite calmly and simply, "Yvonne, Kim is dead." I gasped suddenly, swerved the car as I put my hand to my mouth trying to contain myself, Leonard put his hand on the steering wheel and told me not to worry and just concentrate on the road ahead of me. There he was, my darling husband, consoling me and his daughter had died of a brain tumour. That drive was one of the most difficult drives I had to do.

We managed to get to the hotel safely, we checked in trying to hold it together. Once we got in our room, Leonard was still quite calm and said we needed to let people know and we decided it would be better to text people as we were away and really did not feel like talking to anyone. So there we were texting away and receiving text messages back from loved ones saying how sorry they were, some people even called. Then all of a sudden Leonard began to cry like a baby, I quickly ran over to him and held him in my arms and told him how sorry I was and to just let it all out. I cried with him, I could feel his pain, and was so upset that I would never now meet my step daughter whom I became so fond of. This was probably one of the saddest moments of my life and one that I will never forget. It brought back memories of when Sheralyn a close family friend who was my sisters' best friend, had died of meningitis, which was the first death I had experienced when I was 20.

Morning came and we went down for breakfast, Leonard could hardly eat, although it was no trouble for me, he just wanted to smoke his weed. We then decided that we would forgo our romantic weekend and head home. So we checked out of the hotel early telling the receptionist our reasons, and not even receiving a 'sorry to hear your bad news,' response, we were quite flabbergasted. So began our journey home and the sorrow for the next few months.

Leonard did not want to risk going back to Jamaica before our appeal, although we tried to see if immigration would issue him with a visa due to what had happened. We queued up at the home office in Croydon for hours in the freezing cold clinging onto some sort of hope that they would certainly be compassionate enough to issue him with a visa. Finally we were seen only to be told that they would still not give him a visa under these circumstances, but he could take the risk and go to his daughter's funeral and hope that he would be able to get a visa out there and return to England. We both could not believe their inhumane decision and felt terribly desperate, hopeless and sad. Leonard was not prepared to take that risk at all and so he asked me if I would go and bury his daughter on his behalf. At first, I was a bit fearful of his request, I had not been to Jamaica before and I had not met any members of his family that lived there. He reassured me that I would be fine and that they would look after me.

Thus began the preparations for my trip to Jamaica. Leonard seemed to be taking everything in his stride, forking out money to pay for the funeral and being asked for more and more from Kim's mother. She was becoming quite greedy and callous. Leonard also bought suits for all his sons to wear at the funeral and other items for me to take over for them. I was sad to be leaving my husband behind, even though it was only for one week, but the thought of being without him for one week was too long for me. However, I had to be brave and do this for him, he was relying on me.

He took me to the airport along with his friend Steve and I cried as I went through the barriers, knowing that I would miss him terribly. 'Fix up Yvonne, you're a big girl now,' I said to myself. I was quite anxious on the flight to Jamaica especially after waiting five hours due to delays with the fantastic Air Jamaica. Despite the anxiety the flight was comfortable, roomy seats and decent plane food, consisting of mashed sweet potato and jerk pork, it was yummy and I washed it down with juice and wine. I slept for most of the flight making sure I woke up for the next meal time.

When I arrived in Montego Bay Airport, I was met by Leonard's birth mother, his sister Chanax and her boyfriend. They had a picture of me which had been taken when Leonard and I were married and they were able to recognise me from the photo. They were warm and welcoming, hugging me and asking me about my flight. I felt that I would be ok with them. The drive to New Forest was long and Chanax's boyfriend drove like a maniac along the winding roads, I feared for my life and found his driving skills unbelievable.

I was received in New Forest by Leonard's adopted parents Miss Esmee (who happened to be his great aunt) her husband, and his cousin, the family he grew up with. They too were loving and warm. Leonard's mother kept me by her side throughout my stay in Jamaica except for one occasion when she allowed her granddaughter to take me into Mandeville to visit my grandparents who had since immigrated to Jamaica. Nothing much had changed with them, they were still arguing.

My duty in Jamaica was to hand out more money for several things such as the flowers for the funeral and money to the grave diggers who happened to be Leonard's cousins.

Breakfast in Jamaica was like having dinner, mackerel and green banana, ackee and salt fish with fried dumpling etc etc. I thought I would burst, as my mother-in-law could see I liked my food and was keen to feed me. I also smoked a great deal because I was bored, as my trip to Jamaica was not to have fun but to bury my step daughter. I loved being in Jamaica, as it felt like home in a funny way, the weather was beautiful, even too hot at times which gave me heat rash. However, it was a sad occasion and everyone was melancholy and stressed by the situation.

I went to the funeral parlour with my mother-in-law to pay for the flowers and see Kim lying in her coffin. It was not a pleasant experience; she looked much darker than she did in the many pictures I saw of her albeit she looked at peace. Sadness like none other came over me and I wished that Leonard was here burying his daughter, with me by his side. The funeral was huge, people came from all over and there were many tears, with people wailing at the loss of such a young soul. I had to hold myself together as best I could in order to video the proceedings for Leonard, I found it difficult but did the best I could. My hands shook as I held the tears in trying to video everything. The ceremony was beautiful, especially when Kim's school friends sang and spoke in honour of their friend who had now left them. It was clear that Kim was definitely a special and loving child and would be dearly missed.

After the ceremony, we proceeded to the grave which was amongst the family plot on their land. Leonard's cousin Harry had dug the grave and oversaw the burial. Everyone present was keen to see the goings on and tried to get a prime spot. I was doing my best to video it using the camcorder that I had borrowed. Leonard called to find out how it was all going on and spoke to various members of the family who all tried to console him even though he was inconsolable. When I spoke to him, my heart went out to him, as nothing I could say would take his pain away, it was just heart breaking.

By the time Kim was laid to rest in her grave more tears and wailing were to be heard. There were many flowers and reefs placed on her grave, some included reefs of a teddy bear, her name, daughter, niece etc. It looked very pretty and I ensured I got that on the video so that Leonard would be able to see how pretty her grave looked. When everything was over I was famished and needed to eat, but apparently all the food had finished. Leonard's family told me how people often attended funerals just for the food. I was horrified!

The following couple of days I spent some time with Leonard's sons Brendon and LJ, they were adorable, Brendon was a little chatterbox and a sensitive little soul, whereas LJ was more your rough and tumble type of boy. They were like chalk and cheese and both very good looking, like their dad. I also met Travis, the new child and yes he looked just like Leonard, he was only about 18 months or so and he had his hair plaited in cornrows. My stepsons; I could not help but think, how glad I was that they live here in Jamaica.

I was so relieved when the time came for me to journey back home to my husband and children, it seemed like we were apart for forever even though it was only one week. My kids had stayed with their dad, as Leonard was not in a good enough space to look after them, although he probably could have done with the company. The journey home went smoothly apart from the fact that Air Jamaica in fine Air Jamaica style had cancelled my flight and put me on another flight which meant me having to wait around at Montego Bay airport for three hours or so. I was very agitated and angry that yet again I had to wait around due to Air Jamaica's lax policy on time, so very unprofessional I thought. Miss Esmee had come to the airport with me and a family friend who drove us. She waited around, she was so protective of me, I felt truly blessed that she was my mother-in-law, and I knew that I would miss her.

Arriving back home in England was great, apart from the cold weather. Seeing my children and Leonard again was refreshing. I had felt quite stressed and overwhelmed in Jamaica it was good to be home. Leonard was understandably still very sad and was keen to see the video and it seemed that what I had videoed was not really good enough. However, I tried to be understanding, as it was probably his way of coping with the fact that he was not able to go to the funeral himself.

Chapter 36

Moving On - 2005

Leonard's sadness did not seem to last as long as I expected it would, this could have been due to the fact that his weed intake seemed to double. I often tried to get him to talk about his loss in order to help him come to terms with it; however he was not willing to do this. The following year went by fairly quickly, I was working hard and Leonard worked as and when opportunities arose.

The relationship was a little strained, but I just got on with things the best I could, always offered a listening ear for Leonard if he needed me. In May 2005, more than a year after the death of Kim, the hearing for the appeal came through. Months prior to this, we had been seeing a solicitor, although we found him expensive, we were so desperate to get as much help as possible that we carried on using him. He was located in South London in a pokey little office in an industrial estate, not very professional to say the least! He was recommended by a friend so we felt that he could be trusted despite his look of unprofessionalism.

We turned up at the court both very anxious and nervous. We had organised character references for Leonard in advance and they all met us there, they were my brother Shane accompanied by his girlfriend Kasima, my friends Natalie, Nicola, Hayley and my ex counsellor Mary. I had finished my counselling not long after I met Leonard as I felt I had gone a long enough way with it and had finally attracted the man of my dreams. It was strange for me seeing my counsellor in a different light; she was quite chilled and had a sense of humour. I felt so grateful to have everyone there supporting us.

Just before we were due to go in our solicitor briefed us on how to present ourselves to the judge. Well, I wished he would have taken his own bleeding advice. He was indeed unprofessional! Nerves seemed to get the better of him and I was not impressed, thinking that he had spoilt our chances. It was quite tense and I wanted to speak on behalf of Leonard and Mary, just to make sure that everyone said exactly what they were supposed to say. They did not call upon the character witnesses; they obviously thought their written statements that they had previously sent in were enough. I was very nervous and when it came to my turn to speak even more so; I found the whole ordeal quite intruding, having to speak about all our personal business. The judge called Leonard a charmer which I found a little insulting, Leonard also was very nervous, in fact he looked quite scared. The judge left us feeling quite positive about the outcome which we were to learn about in six weeks' time.

At the end of the ordeal everyone left feeling quite relieved it was all over for now. All but our solicitor and Nicola who had to go back to work went onto a pub for a drink to relax and discuss the events of the morning. It was great for me socialising with Mary. Mary had gone beyond the call of duty for us and I was ever so grateful. Mary enjoyed putting faces to the names of people I had mentioned in my sessions with her. We all had a bit of a laugh over a drink or two before I finally suggested that we perhaps have something to eat, which we did, apart from Mary who had to get back.

For the next six weeks Leonard and I felt like we were living on borrowed time, trying to stay hopeful and positive which proved quite difficult at times. We finally received the letter and we nervously opened it together and read its contents. I could not believe what I was seeing on the pages of A4 paper, I was outraged, which quickly turned into sadness. They had not granted Leonard his visa. They did not seem to care that our case was genuine and that his departure would put unnecessary strain on our family. They had given him a couple of weeks to leave the country in order to apply for his visa from his homeland in Jamaica. Family members and friends that were involved were all informed, they were all sorry to hear the bad news. I started missing him before he had departed, worrying about how I was going to have to cope without him. The few days left before Leonard had to go were spent preparing for him to travel. Leonard seemed to go crazy buying clothes for himself and for his family back home. I felt he was over doing it just a little.

He ended up with four suitcases which I felt was very over the top and totally unnecessary. The impending day arrived when Leonard had to leave, I was extremely distraught, and could not bear the thought of being without my husband for any amount of time. However, there was nothing I could do about the situation and I just had to accept it. I took the day off work to see Leonard off at the airport, and we were accompanied by my loyal brother Shane and his girlfriend Kasima as well as Leonard's friend Steve and his wife Karen who took two of the suitcases. Whilst checking in he had to pay for excess baggage and looking at the check in queue it seemed like most of the passengers travelling to Jamaica would have to be paying for excess baggage. Many of them were repacking their suitcases, trying to even out the kilos in each one. A very typical scenario for people travelling to the Caribbean or Africa!

Leonard seemed somewhat excited about going back home; he was about to see his family whom he had left behind, however he was now leaving me behind and I felt a little indignant. Even Naomi and Adrian were upset to see him go; they had become very fond of him, even to the point of buying him Father's Day cards. We had booked the flights with BA, due to the bad taste that Air Jamaica had left in my mouth. Everything was running smoothly and the flight was on schedule, which I was not too happy about as it meant I had little time with Leonard; Air Jamaica now seemed like a better option. He continued to reassure me that everything would be alright and that he would be back before I knew it. We had decided that, as it could take up to three months to get his visa that I would travel out to be with him for about three weeks.

The time came for us to say goodbye to Leonard and allow him to go through passport control, I hung on to him for dear life, not wanting him to go, however realising that I was a grown woman, I decided to try and control myself. As Leonard wiped my tears away we kissed and he held me for one last time before he had to depart. As he left my heart sunk to the pit of my stomach, I felt like I had been dumped and so alone.

My family and friends at the airport showed me much love and understanding as they all waved goodbye to my dear Leonard. In a zombie like state I walked towards the car park, everything was a little hazy and I asked my brother if he would drive back as I did not think I could manage and would probably end up crashing. During the drive home, Shane and Kasima managed to get me out of the low mood for a short while; however, as I walked into my home, it hit me again just like the cricket ball that had hit me when I was a little girl. I was all alone and the house seemed so empty and dead. I sat on the sofa and cried a little and smoked a little, cried a lot then smoked a lot.

That night I cried myself to sleep, the bed was huge and also empty, and I curled up at the edge of the bed in the foetus position until I fell asleep only to be woken up in the middle of the night by Leonard's call. It was lovely to hear his voice on the other end of the phone, but I felt teased because he was not there with me in the flesh. He had landed safely and was ok. We were like love sick puppies on the phone and this is how it went on every time we spoke.

Hungry for Love

Chapter 37

Coping Alone

The following day I had to go back to work as I had to save as much annual leave as I could for my impending trip to Jamaica to be with my husband. Colleagues were sympathetic and accepted the fact that I was not my usual bubbly self. It was a Friday and there were after work drinks planned, I was not in the mood to attend. However, my colleagues persuaded me to attend, saying that it would do me good to get out. I did not have to worry about the kids' dinner or anything because they were spending the weekend with their dad. The night out was ok, it took a little while for me to feel at ease, but that soon changed with a couple of drinks inside. There was a new guy who took a real liking to me; I quickly informed him that I was married, although still enjoying the attention bestowed upon me.

He seemed like a wild one, but he was funny, he kept buying the rounds, sambuca was the order for the night, and I eventually forgot about my woes. I started to feel sick, a little unsteady on my feet and out of control so I decided to not have any more sambucas, but to stick with vodka. The night carried on till quite late and I enjoyed myself to some degree even

219

though I moaned to everyone that I was really missing my husband.

Once I arrived home, I was on the phone to Leonard, crying at how much I missed him going overboard due to the intoxication. I then managed to cry myself to sleep; this was a regular occurrence. I was not eating properly, however this only lasted a week. I spoke to his aunty who was consoling me and she asked me if I was eating properly, she was concerned for me, I said "Funnily enough, yes." We both found it a little humorous.

After work drinks were always a welcoming thought and I attended as many as possible with present and past colleagues. On one occasion I met up with my friend Sam, she was having drinks with friends at The Fine Line in Canary Wharf. Quite a few of her friends were male and that made the night even more enjoyable. However things got too much for me and my sob story came out about how my husband had been extradited to Jamaica and how much I was missing him. I wish I could change the bleeding record – tears ensued. Big fat tears with me sobbing like a baby – under the influence, of course. Time for me to go home I thought, this just won't do, crying like a baby in front of strangers. Sam was ever so lovely and concerned for me; she walked me to the station to make sure I got on the train safely.

I was finding life difficult, quite a chore to be honest, I had to hold it together at work and come the evenings I was a mess, but still had to put on a brave face in front of the kids. They missed him also, and they probably thought that the sooner he came back the sooner my moods would change. I decided to stop smoking; I found it easy to stop because Leonard wasn't around.

I was continually either on the phone or sending emails to the Jamaican Consulate in Kingston finding out as much information as I could about the status of Leonard's application. They were not giving much away and I became easily frustrated. Before he departed we had painstakingly put together his application in a hard bound A4 folder with all the different legal documents that they required; it was quite a project.

It did not look like they were going to be dealing with his application swiftly as we thought might be the case, the response I received each time was "The application can take up to three months." So my trip to Jamaica was definitely on in order to help reinforce his application. Most of the arrangements for me to come over were pretty much in place. I booked the flight, and brought a few summer clothes, packed my suitcase and packed the kids off to their dads for 3½ weeks, not forgetting to put little notes in their clothes for them to find. Going to Jamaica for the second time in just over a year seemed frivolous. However these trips had been essential and I suppose it would have been nicer to go out there under more favourable circumstances. Anyway, I was very excited about travelling to Jamaica this time round because I was going to see the love of my life and spend three whole weeks and more with him.

I was quite sad to be leaving my children as we had been having lots of fun watching Big Brother together, with Makosi, Science and Derek to name a few of the house members. I told the kids that they would have to update me on the goings on in the house. I gave them a Jamaica calling card each and told them to use it to call me anytime. Onward bound to Jamaica, my brother drove me to the airport and kept my car for his troubles until I was to return with my husband, so I thought...

Chapter 38

Second Honeymoon

Once I arrived in Kingston airport before getting off the plane I went to the toilet and freshened up and went commando. You see, I promised Leonard that I would, so that we could have sex in the car before getting to his mum's house. The thrill I had at the prospect of seeing Leonard was too much for me to handle, I could not believe that it would only be moments now before I would see him. Kingston airport was quite different to Montego Bay, your visitors/greeters had to wait in a particular area which was pretty much outside and I was a little apprehensive. A man approached me and asked me if I wanted him to carry my suitcase, I refused his offer, realising that he would want paying for it.

I struggled a little with my luggage looking for Leonard, and then I spotted him with one leg up on a railing looking tanned and quite boyish – he was seven years younger than me and I felt he certainly looked it now. He was wearing shorts and a vest top. A quick thought ran through my head, 'He looks so young, what am I doing with him?' but I quickly dismissed it. He was still a sight for sore eyes. As we walked towards each other, anticipating our embrace and kiss I became overwhelmed with emotion. As we met, we kissed; his mouth tasted horrible, we then hugged, however, the hug did not last as long as I thought it would, I was crying tears of joy and relief feeling very romantic, but he was a little embarrassed and was not comfortable with displaying his affection in public at that time.

We got my stuff into the boot of the car and once we were inside we had a proper kiss, at which point I told him he would have to stop smoking if he wanted me to be kissing him, I could not bear the taste of his mouth. He said he could not do that and my reaction was, 'Well if you can't beat them join them,' and as he lit up a spliff I decided to have a cigarette. I asked him if we were going to stop off somewhere secluded and reminded him that I had no panties on, he thought I was joking about the whole thing and did not realise that I was going to see it through. He did not want to do it, he said it would feel like he was disrespecting me, my thoughts were 'Please do disrespect me, do you know how long it's been?'

As we drove from Kingston to Mandeville in the hot baking sun, we talked about any and everything whilst I lovingly kept my hand on his leg. I still could not believe that I was with my husband, it was a wonderful feeling. After what seemed like a couple of hours we were driving on the familiar red dusty quiet roads with many pot holes and it was then that I knew we were not far from what would be my home for the next few weeks. We pulled up into the driveway of Leonard's parents' house and it did not seem that long ago that I was there. It was good to see his parents again and I received a warm welcome from them both. His mother had made me something to eat which was good, however what I really wanted was a lovely cup of tea and then spend some quality time, if you know what I mean, with Leonard.

They did not have proper tea so I had to make do with the peppermint tea that I had carried in my handbag; I always had a stash of it due to wind and bloating problems. Leonard showed me our room, and it was not the same one that I had when I had visited them before. This room was on the other side of the house, and I was not too keen on it, as it just seemed somewhat unsafe, with louver windows that did not close, which probably meant all sorts of insects would find their way in. I half unpacked my things and we made up the bed with fresh linen. That night, despite the heat and sweat our lovemaking was out of this world. Leonard was in such ecstasy that he fell off the bed, and I won't mention what it was I was doing to make that happen!

The following morning I was greeted with a breakfast that resembled more of a dinner, it consisted of green banana, yam and mackerel, but me being me, I did not say no. The morning after that we had ackee and salt fish with fried dumpling that Leonard made. Now that was something! The ackees were not from a tin as they are in London, they were fresh and they had a firmer texture, yummy. Breakfasts were like this every day and before long I was putting on weight. However, we did not spend every day at the house...

Our first stop was Montego Bay, where we attended the Reggae Sunsplash, it was great, Damian Marley and Fantasia Barrino were a couple of the guest singers, we had only been able to go to International Day, but it was still a great experience. We had brought a blanket so that we could sit down on the grass when we were tired. We drank rum and coke; Wray and Nephew's rum was dirt cheap; in fact it was the cheapest alcohol you could buy in Jamaica because that it where it was manufactured. Wray and his nephew became our close companions whilst we were in Jamaica. We decided to stay over in Montego Bay but it was rather late for us to find a hotel so we stayed on the beach overnight, it was not as pleasant and romantic as I thought it would be. The night air coupled by the sea breeze meant it was rather chilly and by morning I was quite irritable and desperately needed a bath.

We found a hotel and booked in for one night as we went sightseeing around the area. We went as far as Falmouth where we visited the Green Grotto Cave resort. They charged tourists more than they did the locals. Leonard tried to get me in as a local; however, they looked me up and down and asked me where I came from. At first I was a little stumped but then in the best raw Jamaican accent I could muster up I said, "Me come from New Forest, near Alligator Pond". The teller gave me one look as if to say who are you trying to kid, obviously my accent was not good enough and I was bemused as to how she could bleeding well tell I was not a local. Needless to say we had to pay the tourist fare for me. The following day we drove over to Negril, I always wanted to see the cottage that Gregory Isaacs sang about, but that was not to be. We stayed in a hotel where our room backed out onto the beach, it was heavenly. In the morning we swam in the sea before having breakfast. After which we went back in the sea and enjoyed messing around and then making love in the sea, what a wonderful experience. We drove back home via Black River, I was expecting to see a black river, but the water was a milky colour, so why they called it Black River, I don't know! We stayed back in Mandeville for a couple of days and whilst there we went to Alligator Pond, which was a 15 minute drive, we ate fresh fish which we chose ourselves from their fridge which they cooked on the spot. The food came with bammi and/or festival. The food was exquisite. We went with Leonard's half-brother and family.

It was not long before I became terribly bored at Leonard's parents, their house was so hot and stuffy with loads of insects including the dreaded mosquito; they lived right next to the local water station which meant the air was always damp, perfect environment for them. I had been prepared and brought my anthisan cream with me in case I got bitten. By the end of the holiday I had to buy another tube of cream as I was pulverised by mosquitoes, it was so bad that it spoilt my holiday. I was forever applying the cream to practically every part of my body. Even though we slept with a net over our bed they still managed to get me in my sleep. I would cover over, suffering the heat, only to wake up and find I was even bitten on my face. Along with the heat rash which seemed to worsen whenever I drank alcohol I don't know how I got through the holiday, I wished I could have left my skin back in England.

Off we went for our second excursion, this time we headed for Ochi Rios, we booked into a hotel for two nights and we went to Dunns River Falls, now that was a beautiful experience, the cool falling water beating on my body felt like I was getting a massage. The Falls and the surrounding area were amazing. Leonard had decided to take our camera to take photos, I did not think it was wise as we were going in water, but he insisted and said he would make sure he held it above the water. We took some lovely photos and I was really looking forward to seeing them. Well before long as we descended down the Falls,

Leonard forgot that he had the camera and it went under the water. I was very annoyed, as it was not a cheap camera and I really wanted to see the photos, I found it hard to accept that it was not going to happen. I could not help but think, 'What an idiot for bringing the camera anyway.'

Come the evening we went to a beach party, again, it was a brilliant experience, the sun setting in the background, warm breeze, dancing on the beach with the sand slipping through our toes, I had a lot of fun drinking and dancing. I slept well that night and the hotel room was very comfortable with suitable air conditioning. The following day we decided to chill out on the beach, the hotel was all inclusive and we ordered our drinks as early as 11.00am we were drinking daiquiris, which were like cocktails but with loads of crushed ice, similar to our slush puppies, but obviously with alcohol. My favourite was the pinna-colada daiquiri although this did not stop me from experimenting with other flavours. There were many hustlers on the beach, which became a little annoying at times. Leonard bought me a shell bracelet and matching earrings which I still have to this day. There was a guy selling hash cake and Leonard asked me if I wanted some, I thought it was a good idea, especially as I love cake and was on holiday after all. I ate the slab of cake quite quickly and waited for something to occur, but nothing happened and I assumed that the cake was rubbish, but resigned myself to the fact that it tasted nice and that was good enough for me.

What followed was probably one of the funniest or frightening experiences of my life, depending on how you look at it. I fell asleep on the beach, lucky enough to be in the shade. I went into a dreamy state and was half asleep, as certain people walked pass me, my thoughts were no longer my own, I blurted out what I was thinking without my prior knowledge. I know it sounds weird, however, after realising that I had just heard my voice, in a confused state I would then ask Leonard if I had just said anything, and his response was "Yes," always accompanied by a grin or a laugh. After a few times of this happening, I started to panic, my head started to spin and run away with me at the same time. I was not in charge of my thoughts and I felt completely out of control and then started sweating profusely. I was literally going out of my mind and was petrified.

Enough was enough! I demanded that Leonard take me up to our room so I could sleep this shit off, as I could not cope with this feeling. First, I needed to have a shower before I could lie in the bed, so I asked Leonard if he would not mind washing me down. He obliged, laughing whilst doing so, I was not finding this funny at all and then all of a sudden I started to cry and it was as if my mind had gone way back in time and I was now Yvonne the little girl, accusing Leonard of molesting me and sobbing "I am going to tell my mummy" and "I want my mummy." I was bewildered and seething with anger whilst Leonard continued to laugh at my little scene, he somehow managed to calm me down, dry me off and put me to bed, he also made me a cup of tea and stayed with me until I fell asleep, I was still livid. I slept for hours and when I awoke I felt better but not 100% and said "Never again." Nothing more was said about this, whilst on holiday.

We drove along the coast past, Port Maria, Buff Bay, Port Antonio, and Morant Bay the views were absolutely exquisite. We even visited the famous blue lagoon in Portland, and that was a sight, deep blue water in a secluded spot. The devil in me wanted to go in the lagoon not wanting to believe that it was bottomless, but I thought better of it. We stopped off in Boston famous for its jerk pork, people were surprised to see a Rasta buy pork, but Leonard was buying it for me and I sure weren't a Rasta despite my locks, and boy did it taste good, although a little too peppery for me.

We went back to New Forest for a couple of days and visited Lovers Leap a high cliff where two slaves jumped 1700ft into the sea below because they were being forced apart. That was a romantic time we spent together looking way down into the Caribbean Sea below wondering what it would have been like for the two love birds. We drove to my parents' home town in St Thomas and visited the famous Baths. The water running out of the rocks was hot and we spent half the day relaxing and enjoying the baths. Due to its healing properties people were there trying to cure their ailments and we saw a young girl who was riddled with chicken pox hoping that it would clear her spots away.

My trip to Jamaica was a holiday of a lifetime, Leonard made sure about that. We drove around the whole of Jamaica, touching every single parish. In between enjoying ourselves we also became quite anxious about the fact that we had still not heard anything about Leonard's visa, we wrote emails and made phone calls and still nothing. My time was running out and I was starting to feel quite depressed.

One evening at Leonard's parents' home, I went to the loo, as you do, and after washing my hands I dried them off with my flannel, the memory of what happened to me is actually causing my fingers to tremble right now and stopping me from typing properly! I felt something prick my finger, but it did not feel like a pin prick it felt like a fucking great needle prick! I threw down the flannel only to see some long, grey looking ugly creature crawl from it. At this point I started to cry and scream just like a baby, holding my finger out and shouting for Leonard to come and help me. I could not even look at my finger as I became hysterical, jumping and sobbing because I was in complete agony. Leonard came running to the rescue asking me what happened, he went to see what had bitten me and apparently it was something called a 40 leg, and I presume it was called that because it had 40 fucking legs! Oh how I hated that thing. My finger had doubled in size by now and had turned a bright red colour. Leonard called his mum to find out what he should do and even suggested taking me to the hospital, but she said he did not need to do that. He then proceeded to squeeze the poison from my finger, causing me even more pain. His mother rushed home from the shop to tend to me, they bandaged my finger and gave me some pain killers. I was bloody well traumatised.

On our travels I had brought what Jamaicans call a 'wash out' from a Rasta in May Pen, it has the same effect as laxatives. I drank a bit of the herbal remedy on a daily basis hoping it would do me some good and get rid of all the toxins in my body. I was visiting the toilet regularly which is what I wanted, and even though it was painful at times I still kept taking it to the point where my stools were runny and pretty much non-existent. Whenever I ate I would need to run straight to the toilet.

Leonard's mum and dad had promised to kill one of their pigs for me and three days before I was due to go home, they did just that. I watched while they slaughtered the pig which was carried out in a humane way, nonetheless it was still distressing for me to see. They skinned it too and it was all over so quickly, this was all done by Ms Esmee's brother. The meat was cooked on the same day ready for me to eat for my dinner. I had never tasted pork as sweet as that. The meat was soft and it tasted nothing like the pork from England, all I can say is that it went down well.

Two days before I was due to leave, I had already started missing Leonard; I was refusing to accept that his visa would not be ready by the time I was leaving. I so wanted us to be travelling back home to London together and I held onto that hope. All of a sudden I started to feel an excruciating pain in the left side of my lower stomach. I tried to grin and bear it, but it progressively got worse to the point where I was in tears. The pains were very much like contractions, as they came and went every few minutes or so and they had the same intensity. We went to the chemist to buy some pain killers; however, they did not work. I became desperate and could no longer handle the pain. Leonard was sympathetic and was very worried for me and decided to take me to see a doctor.

I was finally called in after about an hour wait and met the doctor, who asked me questions about myself and asked me to go on the scales. In my head, I thought to myself, 'Why are you weighing me? What the hell has my weight got to do with anything, the pain is in my stomach?' I was to get up on the couch whilst he examined my abdomen, I was a little apprehensive about having to show my bare stomach full of stretch marks and I forgot that I had worn my hen night red g-string which said 'Devil' on the front of them, I instantly felt ashamed. He wrote down notes about me and my symptoms and said he was not sure what was wrong and could not diagnose me. So he wrote a letter referring me to the hospital. I read the letter as we left the surgery and he referred to me as obese. 'How very dare he?' I thought.

We drove off to the hospital and as I walked through the hospital I could not help but think, I don't want to get treated here, it was nothing like the hospitals in England. However, I was in agony and needed to get rid of this pain. The wait was long, there were so many people in front of us and I could envisage us being there all day. But to my surprise, I was called in sooner than I expected, probably due to the fact that I was from England and had insurance. The doctor was a young woman, nice enough and after reading the letter, examining me and asking me questions she informed me that it was likely my appendix, she arranged for me to have a scan to confirm this and was preparing a bed for me. She gave us a form for the scan and told us to wait outside. In the short space of time Leonard said "Hell no, let's get out of here, you can see a doctor in England, I am not letting these people cut you open, they just want your money because you are English." At that, we were off making our way back to our car and home. Leonard tried to console me as much as he could and told me not to worry as it was only one more day before I was to leave to go home. I had to trust him on this one.

I don't know what it was that caused that pain, whether it was the fresh pork the 'wash out' or the poison from the 40 leg, or a combination of all three, but luckily on the day I was due to leave the pain had eased off a bit. That day I was not a happy bunny, I still had some hope that Leonard would be coming home with me but it was not to be. As I packed to go home without much effort or energy I cried. Leonard helped me pack my things and he had an extra suitcase full of food, ackee, buns, breadfruit, lobster, mangoes and rum for me to take home.

After saying my goodbyes to Leonard's family, Leonard dropped me off to the airport; the drive to Kingston was long and depressing, as it was raining quite heavily at one point which caused a lot of traffic to build up. Once there, I checked in which was a bit laborious, my suitcases were opened up and checked which did not please me in the slightest. The woman seemed obsessed with a quart of rum that I had in my suitcase, she kept shaking it and watching the bubbles disperse, and I thought 'What the hell is her fascination with my rum?' Only to find out that people plant drugs in liquid form in those bottles. I could not believe what I was hearing. Anyway everything was clear and they checked me in and hauled my suitcases away where I would meet them in England.

Saying goodbye to Leonard was awfully painful. I could not bear it, however, he reassured me that it would not be long before he would be home as the maximum amount of time it could be was four weeks now. This kind of gave me some solace and despite the trauma with the 40 leg centipede, my contractions, my skin being constantly inflamed, oh and the hash cake saga, I did not want to leave Leonard. We kissed and cuddled and said our goodbyes and I had to hold it together as I walked through customs, 'I am a big woman, so stop behaving like a child,' I said to myself once again. I slept for most of the flight to numb out my pain, but as ever making sure I woke up at meal times.

On the other side of the Atlantic it was good to be home albeit without my husband. I was exhausted and by now my stomach pains had subsided with just a little twinge here and there. As I walked through to passport control, there were police men with sniffer dogs walking towards us and one of the police men commanded his dog to come over and sniff me out. I was a little scared and offended and thought, 'Is it because of my locks?' The dog sniffed me out alright, concentrating on my private area, I was totally embarrassed. 'They thought I had drugs in my fanny did they? Huh! It sure weren't their lucky day,' I thought to myself as I walked away.

Chapter 39

Home Alone... Again

Arriving home was good, even after a second honeymoon in Jamaica with the man of my dreams, there was no place like home. No insects to bother me for a start. However, I was missing my man terribly, but had to hold myself together as it couldn't be much longer before he would join me.

It was great being reunited with my children and they were also pleased to see me as well as excited about the gifts I had brought back for them. They were a bit aggrieved that I had left them with their dad, as they preferred to be with me. Their half- sister had died when I was away, she was still born, and I felt a little guilty that I was not there to comfort them.

I was back at work within no time and it was not good to be there. I had to wear foundation because the skin around my nose had literally burnt off due to sunburn – yes black people burn in the sun too! Everyone at work expected that Leonard had flown back with me, and I felt awfully embarrassed to tell them that he was still there. I threw myself into work in order to not feel so bad. I missed Leonard's cooking, especially when I got home from work, and I could not really go out much for after work drinks, because Leonard was not around to look after the kids, although I went when their dad took them on the Tuesday and Thursday evening.

Leonard and I had our regular phone calls and each time I would ask him if he heard from the British Embassy in Kingston and the answer was always the same. Then one day whilst going about my normal business, I got the call – the call which made me jump for joy! Leonard's visa had come through three weeks after I had left Jamaica. The joy I felt in my heart was immense. I had to call BA to change his flight details and this costs me £100, but that was no issue at all. He was due to arrive back in London at 10.00am in a couple of days' time. I booked the day off in order to pick him up from the airport. I was excited.

It was an overnight flight and one of Leonard's brothers was due to take him to Kingston airport. I called him on the hour every hour to see how he was getting on with packing, saying his goodbyes etc etc. At the allotted time that his brother was due to pick him up he had not arrived yet, which caused both Leonard and I a lot of anxiety. His brother felt he did not need to leave as early as Leonard wanted him to, he stood his ground and picked Leonard up one hour later than the time Leonard asked him to. He came by with a laid back attitude insisting that they had more than enough time to get to the airport. When Leonard informed me about this I was not happy, but what could I do? I just sat back and prayed that everything would be ok.

As I lay in my bed trying to sleep I got a call from Leonard to say that he had missed his flight. I could not believe what I was hearing, I was absolutely enraged! Leonard felt like he had let me down and was very upset. He said that the next BA flight would be two days later at the same time, but I was not happy with that, I could not and would not wait that long. All that anticipation! I asked Leonard to check if there were any earlier flights and the only earlier flight was a Virgin flight which left in 8 hours. Leonard was happy to wait for the next BA flight, but I certainly was not. I wanted my husband back with me as soon as possible. So I impulsively booked that flight and put it on the credit card £600!

I decided to go into work rather than waste a day's holiday, and asked for the following day off, which was fine. Everyone was surprised to see me and I explained to them what had happened. I was in stress mode! I left work early and made my way to the airport on the tube to meet my husband. I arrived in good time and waited patiently eating snacks and popping out for cigarettes to ease the anxiety (not so patiently, in hindsight).

His plane had landed and I was gripped with fear and excitement at the same time. I waited at the barrier for him to come through the doors; I was there for a long time watching all the passengers come through and no sign of Leonard. Fear took hold even more because the passengers from his flight were dwindling and then they finally stopped and Leonard was nowhere to be seen. Had he missed the plane again? Did they send him back? I did not know what to do except call him and the first few times it went straight through to his voicemail. I wanted to cry and scream and throw my toys out of the pram. 'Where the fuck was he? Why was this happening to me? Didn't they know how much I needed him?' My mobile started ringing, and it was him, I quickly answered and Leonard informed me that he was here, but they were just questioning him and they wanted to ask me a few questions to verify that he was my husband and I was expecting him. I sighed with relief and assured the woman at the other end of the phone of this and then he hung up.

Still feeling anxious and needing to see him with my own two eyes before I could relax, I waited a few more minutes and then there he was strolling through the doors with his three suitcases on a trolley. He was wearing one of his Rastafarian hats with the Lion of Judah on it. His locks all tucked in securely inside the hat and high upon his head. As before, he was a sight for sore eyes. He made a bit of a scene as he came through the doors, chanting "Burn Babylon," "Justice for I and I Rasta from the tribe of Judah." He was drawing a lot of attention to himself and I was a little embarrassed, but he did not care, he was angry with the way he had been treated and felt justified in trying to cause a bit of a scene. I walked over to him as quickly as my legs could carry me. His embrace felt like heaven and as we kissed it felt fantastic for me to be in his arms once more. We made our way to the tube, struggling with suitcases and bags that he had. I was on cloud nine and felt whole again now that my man was with me.

Chapter 40

Happy 30th Leonard

Life soon got back to normal. I was delighted with my life, my children seemed happy and I certainly was. Leonard's birthday was approaching and I felt it would be nice to throw him a surprise birthday party. I did not have much time to organise it, but I roped in my friends, in particular, Marcia to help me. I got in touch with all his mates to ensure that they would be there as well as my friends, some of which helped to prepare food. It was quite a hectic time for me, but I knew it would be worth it.

Leonard made the most of his birthday, and started drinking quite early in the day and smoking his weed. We arranged to go out for a meal so that Marcia could go round and set up the house ready for the surprise for Leonard. He very nearly spoiled everything because he passed out due to the alcohol and weed before we were ready to go for the meal. I was very exasperated with him and upset, thinking that all my plans were going to pot (excuse the pun). I managed to sober him up and get him ready for the meal which went ok, but could have been nicer. My mind was on the party and I worried about how they were doing and if everything was going to schedule. Leonard was trying very hard to make an effort especially as he had overdone it earlier in the day.

I got the phone call to say that everything was set so we made our way home without Leonard having any clue about what was going on. As we walked up to the house, I could see that Leonard was clueless and I was excited. I made sure I opened the door and as we walked into the dark house, I let him walk into the living room first and there everyone was. "Surprise!" they all shouted. Leonard was astounded, and I was so chuffed with myself that it all worked out. We both gave speeches, Leonard told his friends off for not telling him and I thanked everyone for their help in making the surprise happen and I spoke about my love for Leonard and how much he meant to me, everyone in unison said, "Ahh" when they heard me speak.

The party was fun, friends and some family members around, lots of food and drink and good music. Leonard was really happy that I put on the party for him, and funnily enough he ended up being the host for his own party. I was never a very good host, I always wanted to enjoy myself at my own parties and Leonard did not mind serving his guests. The party went on until about 4.00am, I was hoping that it would carry on a bit longer like my parties of old, but it was not to be.

Barry and Pet, Leonard's best pal and his wife stayed and we all stayed up late drinking and laughing about this and that. They kipped on the sofa and in the morning, well afternoon, helped us clean up.

Weeks later, Leonard and I saw some photos of the party and I was stunned at how we both looked, the only description I could use is 'FAT'. I was now at least a size 18/20. Yes we looked happy, but I wondered how our bed coped with the two of us. I did not realise we had both put on so much weight.

Life was good, we did shopping together, went out dancing together, we were enjoying being with each other and were very much in love. Going clubbing with my husband was great for me; it was so much nicer than going out with the girls, although I did go out with my friends occasionally, a girls night out was always in order.

Chapter 41

Downhill - 2006

Leonard's jobs started to come in drips and drabs not like how it used to be. He had also fallen out with Linford by now and I was glad in a way as Linford was a bad influence on Leonard, he had brought a huge stash of weed into my house once and was about to cut it up into tiny portions to sell. "Not in my house," I told him in no uncertain terms. The dry lining jobs had dried up and the painting and decorating jobs were few and far between. It was a little frustrating for me and I started to become a little resentful that I was once again a breadwinner.

Things between us were changing and it all seemed to start when Leonard started going out a lot more with his mates down to The Lamb, the local pub and then onwards to a club in Dalston most Friday's. I started to feel very uncomfortable with this which I communicated to him, he was not happy with what I had to say and he told me that he needed to go out with his friends. I recognised that I was probably being a bit too needy and told him not to worry about me and I would deal with my issues of neediness. However, Leonard started to go out more often and when I approached him about it again, his response was "Me is a big blood claart man, and me will go out whenever I please," in his Jamaican accent. The way he spoke made me feel uneasy so I decided that there was not much I could do, and I started to go out with my friends whenever he went out. He then complained about going out with me, because my friends were always there, and he did not always feel comfortable going to the posh venues. He never complained before so I assumed he was fine with that.

Leonard's weed smoking escalated and I disliked this very much, as he always wanted me to drive him to Hackney Wick in order to buy his weed from his regular supplier. Even though I did not want to do this I complied, it just made for a peaceful life; he was very grumpy when he did not have his weed. I was very concerned with the amount of weed he was smoking, and tried to talk to him about it, but he was not interested in what I had to say. I felt that he was blocking out the death of Kim, it seemed like he had not really mourned her death.

Our conversations dwindled, Leonard just did not want to talk much like we used to. He kept pushing me away and I could not cope with this, but did not know what to do. I spoke to my friends about this and some of my colleagues, who offered support and advice. My friend and colleague Lorraine, was a tower of strength at this time, she did not tell me what to do, but just helped me to have an open mind, she was very subtle in her approach.

I threw myself into my work and did lots of overtime, something that I never really did or even believed in as I did not really like my job by now. However, the extra money came in handy and I felt it was better than being at home with a guy who hardly spoke to me and was not emotionally available to me. I even lied a few times to say I was working late, but really went out for drinks after work.

I often got home drunk, but tried to hide it from the children, as I did not want them to see me drunk. Most times I managed to hide it, so I thought, and sometimes they were already in bed by the time I got home, and my dinner was always there. Some mornings I woke up still feeling very merry, but by the time I got to work, I had a hangover and needed a big fry up in order to get through the morning.

I worked hard and took on extra duties that enabled me to work towards a promotion and come out of the secretarial field once and for all. It was not easy but I was determined. I applied for a couple of jobs but unfortunately did not get them. One of the guys that I was up against was a colleague, Dominic who sat opposite me and we got on very well, in fact we often had a real good laugh. He was successful and even though I was disappointed for myself I was glad that he got the job and not someone else. My main boss Mark, a lovely down to earth guy backed me 100% and encouraged me to study for the IMC (Investment Management Certificate). I decided to do so and found it very difficult; I felt as if I was out of my depth but with mentoring from Lorraine I did not give up. I studied hard and found that I was smoking a great deal more in order to try and stay focussed.

I struggled with the math and felt so inferior. I asked a colleague Rachel for help, she had a maths degree and was very intelligent. She was very helpful. I did not feel confident that I would pass the exam. I did the mock test online and was averaging pretty good marks. So I took the exam, I hate exams especially if maths is involved. It was excruciating and needless to say I failed miserably. I was upset, and a little embarrassed because everyone else seemed to pass, so why couldn't I?

I was also having nightmares on a regular basis by now; I could never remember the content, however. Leonard would wake me up and ask me what was wrong, I did not have a clue why he was asking me this in the middle of the night, and as far as I was concerned I was asleep and perfectly ok. But he informed me that I was kicking violently in my sleep. This I was not aware of, until finally the kicking started to wake me up. There were times when I woke up frightened by the vicious kicking I would do in my sleep. It confused me because I could not tell you what I was dreaming about. This happened on a regular basis. Clearly something was disturbing me.

Chapter 42

Body Image

My weight was getting me down; it was creeping up and I was now a size 20, even though I would not admit that I was that large, I still tried to squeeze into smaller sizes, as long as they had Lycra. I refused to wear baggy clothes because they made me look even bigger. I often went out shopping for clothes, and would not try them on before I bought them, only to find that when I returned home they did not fit. Instead of taking them back and exchanging them for a bigger size I would throw them in the back of the wardrobe in the hope that I would lose some weight and get into them, alas it never happened.

Yet again I was so depressed about my weight I did not know what to do. I tried cutting down on food, and when I went out for drinks I would have vodka and slim line tonic, which tasted quite disgusting. But it was called the slimmer's drink, so that's what I had most of the time.

My friend at work Kate had a boob job and she was now feeling a lot more confident about herself. She went to Harley Street to get them done. I thought about going, not to get a boob job because I was a size 38H, so did not need that in the slightest, but a tummy tuck or liposuction would be good I thought. I booked an appointment at the Transform clinic in Harley Street and was very excited at the prospect of having my tummy reduced and finally looking a lot better than I did. But my excitement was short lived, I was told that I was obese and would need to lose weight before they even considered me for a tummy tuck. Obese; I was tired of hearing that word to describe me. Yes I was overweight, but I wasn't all flabby, I carried my weight pretty well. I wanted to cry, my dream of having a flat stomach shattered in seconds. I was advised that the only thing they could do for me was to fit me with a gastric band which cost £7,000 and they offered the finance for it. I found the woman somewhat patronising and not very genuine at all. I considered getting it done, thinking that this was the only option for me. However after much consideration and thinking about how that woman made me feel I decided not to go ahead with it, besides I could not really afford it.

I then heard about Paul McKenna and how he was able to 'Make you thin.' I did some internet research and found out that he had a 70% success rate which thrilled me so booked onto one of his seminars. I found it to be a great experience; he did group hypnosis and gave us positive affirmations. I learnt new techniques on how to eat, like chewing many times, putting my knife and fork down in between mouthfuls, stopping when I'm full and not restricting what I want to eat. All these techniques made a lot of sense and with the hypnosis I felt that I had finally found the answer to my weight problems. I came out of there feeling on top of the world and extremely confident.

I put into practise what I had learned and it seemed to work, I managed to lose a stone and a bit and then everything seemed to fall apart, for some reason I could no longer keep it up. I was one of the 30% that Paul McKenna could not make thin. I was bewildered, upset and depressed. I resigned myself to the fact that I would always be fat.

I would use laxatives whenever I overate and felt bloated and my usage of them increased. There were times when my stomach ached tremendously the morning after, but I did not care, I wanted a flat stomach and could not achieve this with exercise. But who was I kidding, the laxatives did not give me a flat stomach either, although they got rid of the bloating. They also created a vicious cycle because once my bowels were emptied, I then felt ravenous and would just eat more food and then take more laxatives.

Chapter 43

Alcoholic?

In September 2006 I felt that I had had enough of being married to Leonard, the marriage was going downhill and I no longer felt fulfilled or happy. I told him that we should split and he was not having any of it. It was a painful conversation and I cried pretty much all the way through. He said he could understand because he had not been working towards his goal of becoming a dentist and he knew that I married him because he was ambitious. He promised that he would start working harder and do whatever it took for us to stay together, even to the point of allowing me to cut his locks off if I wanted to. I tested him on that one and got a pair of scissors and went to cut them off, but he would not let me, and I thought to myself, 'All mouth!' Against my better judgement, I decided to give him a chance and work at the marriage.

In October Leonard had to have a fairly routine operation. He had to stop smoking the weed two weeks prior to this which he was able to do, however I noticed that he would drink a shot of brandy or rum in the morning, which he claimed was to clear his chest as he felt he had a cold coming on. I was a little suspicious of this. In the two weeks of him not smoking, he changed considerably. He was a lot grumpier and for the first time since his daughter died, he spoke about it and told me that he felt guilty about not being there for her before she died. I was happy to listen and felt relieved that he was now talking about it, I even mentioned to him that this was the first time he had spoken about it and it was because he was not blocking out his emotions with the weed.

There was a documentary on the TV about a rap star who stopped smoking weed, they documented his battle to give it up and as I sat and watched it, I thought Leonard would find it interesting and tried to get him to watch it. But he shouted and cursed and refused to watch it, saying he did not need to. I was stunned by his attitude. Due to his moodiness at not being able to smoke, ironically I could not wait for him to be able to start smoking again. Without his weed he was not the nice guy I had fallen in love with. I supported him whilst he had his operation as he was very fearful of needles and the whole experience. I nursed him back to health and tried to carry on with life.

Going out for work drinks was still the order of the day, I enjoyed it, it was a means of escape for me especially as drinks were always flowing. On one occasion we went to the Drunken Monkey in Shoreditch, in fact this was the second time we had gone to this venue. I loved their mojito cocktails and had by now consumed four and ready to have my fifth one which Nial had bought for me. However, after a couple of sips Nial advised me that I should not continue drinking it because, "Your eyes look funny," he said. I told him there was nothing wrong with me, I hadn't drunk as much as I normally had, and could see no problem. He insisted that I did not look right and that I should not drink anymore. I reluctantly gave into him and decided not to finish my drink and seconds later I fell asleep at the table, or as others would say, 'I passed out.' I did not know how long I was out for until somebody woke me up, I was startled and lost all my bearings, I stumbled out of my seat and became frantic and unsteady on my feet, I was having the shakes and before I knew it, I vomited the entire contents of my stomach up onto a nearby bag and jacket that were on the floor beside me, they belonged to Nial! Oops!

Colleagues gathered around me trying to help, I was still very unsteady and lost control of my body and mind, it was an awful experience. My colleagues were very concerned, trying to steady and calm me down and I even started to cry. They called Leonard and asked if he could pick me up as they were quite worried about me. Leonard could not pick me up because he had not applied for his British license yet, so they ordered a taxi. However, the taxi driver took one look at me and refused to take me. They pleaded with him that I was not drunk and just sick and he still refused. Then Zara asked him if she accompanied me in the taxi would he take me then, at which point he agreed. So the taxi drove me home with Zara making sure that I was ok. When we arrived Zara called Leonard to meet me outside our house and then Zara carried on in the taxi all the way to Wimbledon. Leonard put me straight to bed.

Christmas 2006 – I was excited about all the parties and drinking that I would be able to do. Team drinks, team dinner, departmental dinner and dance, clubbing with friends, the works – I really looked forward to them all.

The department dinner and dance was held on a boat at the embankment and it was a James Bond theme. I managed to find a posh long dress big enough for me to fit into at Font Hill Road. Marcia accompanied me to buy it and her input was valuable. I was pleased with my dress it was a shimmering burgundy colour with soft pleats and nipped in at the waist to the front of the dress. It came with a diamante broach at the bust line. It was too long so I went to my mum's to use her sewing machine and take it up a couple of inches. I accessorised it with long black velvet gloves, dangling diamond earrings and a diamond ring with a bracelet attached to it which I wore over the gloves. I also bought an old fashioned cigarette holder, which I thought would look quite classy and very much in line with the James Bond theme.

The night was fun, we had our meal, and even though I managed to feel slightly comfortable at the table I could not wait for the disco. I was one of the first people on the dance floor, the music was not really to my liking, and however, I was tipsy enough to not let that spoil my night. After some time the alcohol started to wear off so I walked around the tables emptying what was left in the bottles of wine into my glass – it was mainly red wine that was left over. By the end of the night I no longer looked like a classy James Bond character, I had fallen off a chair, ripped the hem of my posh dress, needed help getting off the boat, and was put in a taxi by Reena and Daresh who told the taxi man to ring them once he had dropped me off, that's how worried they were about me. Lorraine had offered to take me home earlier, but I was not ready and wanted to go on elsewhere with the others, which was not to be now, due to my drunken state. By the time I got home I stumbled to the kitchen and propped myself up on the worktop, called Leonard on the phone to come and get me. He wanted to know where I was and I simply replied "In the kitchen." He went downstairs to assist me up the stairs, being the size I was and the state I was in he found it difficult. He managed to get me to the top of the stairs and accidently – or was it on purpose? – let me go, at which point I fell on my bottom and slid back down the stairs with my bottom hitting each step along the way. By now Leonard had had enough of me coming home drunk, so I resigned myself to the fact that I would have to manage by crawling up the stairs on my own.

Chapter 44

Reality Check - 2007

I was becoming more and more depressed, crying all the time and finding life stressful. I went to see the doctor at work, and as soon as I opened my mouth I started to cry, I could hardly get the words out. The doctor was very sympathetic and prescribed me antidepressants, which I was not too keen to go on again. She said it was just to help me cope with work and life, so I agreed. She told me to come back to her in a couple of weeks to see how I was. I told Leonard that I was given antidepressants and I did not get much of a response and no real sympathy. On my second visit to the doctor I felt a little better but not much, the doctor was keen to find out why I often got depressed. I told her briefly about how I was feeling in my marriage and how I found it impossible to lose weight which often got me down, so she referred me to a psychiatrist.

In the meantime work was also becoming a pain; it seemed like two of my bosses had it in for me, always wanting to know my every move, wanting me to do menial tasks and piling on the work, some of it unnecessary. I was not enjoying sex anymore; I think the tablets affected my libido. It had become a regular occurrence that I had to fight Leonard off me, although sometimes I would just give in. Nevertheless, on one particular occasion he just would not take no for an answer, I insisted that I did not want sex and he insisted that he did. I became so tired of fighting him off and eventually Leonard climbed on top of me and did his thing. As he thrust back and forth I just laid there like a plank of wood, somehow I took my mind away from what was happening and did not participate, he, however, carried on regardless. When he finished the deed, I said to him, "I can't believe you just did that," his response was, "Don't worry, it won't happen again." But the way he said it was as if I had done something wrong. I felt totally used and abused. 'Was that not what they call marital rape?'

My appointment came for me to see the psychiatrist in Harley Street and the appointment lasted for about an hour and twenty minutes. I waited anxiously in the posh waiting room; I had never seen a psychiatrist before. I wasn't mad, that I knew, but I started to doubt myself. He was a strange looking man with a slight pot belly and dirty looking glasses; he looked very deeply into my eyes as if he was searching my soul. He asked me many questions about my past, my depression, weight, marriages etc etc. He then said he needed to refer me to a therapist and gave me a choice of a male or female, he said the male was a very straight to the point kind of person. I was apprehensive but thought maybe it would be good for me to see a male therapist and decided to see him, his name was David and he also worked in Harley Street. I felt very honoured that I was probably seeing the best people in their field but concerned that I still needed to see a therapist after all the counselling I had had with Mary.

Back at work I was reprimanded by one of my bosses, whom I felt was being a bit of a bully as he knew I was seeing a doctor and having problems. At this point I felt I could no longer take anymore. I managed to hold the tears in until I went to the toilet and then the tears were just overflowing. For some strange reason I felt quite traumatised and did not know where to turn. I spoke to Kate and Lorraine and they could not believe the state I was in. They called the office manager and I went to see her in a private meeting room and the tears could not stop. 'What the hell was happening to me?' I was sent home in a taxi and signed off for a week.

Chapter 45

You're an Addict

Seeing David was probably the best thing that could have happened to me. I gave him a synopsis of my life and at the end I added, "Oh, and I just can't seem to lose weight, no matter what I do." His words were, "That's because you're an addict." I felt so insulted, how dare he call me that. I did not do drugs, what the hell was he talking about? Unbeknown to me David was an Addiction Therapist and he explained to me that I was a food and sugar addict and that was why I could not lose weight. As I pondered over his words, they seemed to make a little sense. He told me to go to a twelve step fellowship for overeaters to see if it would help and also told me not to eat sugar and white flour and to have only three meals a day with nothing in between and he would see me next week. At the end of the session as I was about to leave, he told me that no one leaves this room without getting a hug first. I was a little surprised because Mary never hugged me after our sessions, what was this man after? Well, let me tell you, that man opened his arms and held me like I have never been held before and hugged me. I felt really cared for and loved unconditionally from that hug, it actually made me burst into tears. I was confused.

I went back to work the following week and did the best I could. My boss apparently felt really bad and started to tread a little carefully around me. Damn right! I had always found authority figures hard to deal with especially if they dared reprimand me. Leonard and I were becoming more and more distant, I would try and talk to him about my sessions and what I had learned about myself and tried to encourage him to see someone also, but he was not interested and continued to go out and do his own thing.

I did as David suggested and went to the meeting which was strange but interesting; I spoke about how I could not imagine my life without cake. I tried to follow the food plan he had given to me. To my surprise I could not stick to it and could not understand why. It was proving very difficult. I went back to see him a week later and we spoke some more about my past and I cried in the session. I told him I could not follow the food plan properly. He quite casually said, "Don't worry, just keep trying." There was no pressure, which I liked. The fact that I could not do it made me think a lot about the fact that maybe I was an addict, although I could not believe that I was once again in therapy after having seven years with Mary.

One night Leonard and I had both gone out separately, I got home around 4.00am and he did not get home until 7.00am and when he did arrive home, he seemed very alert and would not come to bed. I thought it was strange and asked him why he would not come to bed as he must surely be tired. He said he had not long drunk a red bull and was not feeling sleepy. That morning he had packed a change of clothes to go out straight after work, this I also thought was a little bizarre as he had never done that before, however, he said that he and the guys were all getting changed at one of their houses and then going out. Do men do that?

Things were getting worse between Leonard and I. He had started to hog his phone, and would not let it out of his sight. One day he was relaxing in the bath and it rang, I asked him if he wanted me to get it for him and he hastily said no. I was already near the phone so reached for it to hand it to him and before I could turn around Leonard had jumped out of the bath and snatched the phone from me. I made it clear that I was not going to answer it, only trying to hand it to him. It was then that I started to become very suspicious. I had started talking to a male friend Julian on the phone that I had met years before, it was probably wrong of me, but I did not hide the fact from Leonard, besides he was a good listener. I wanted to talk to a man so I could get a male's viewpoint on the problems I was encountering with my husband. My therapist? Oh! He was gay. I was even flirting a lot with guys at work; it was a good distraction from my problems and my boredom at work.

I started to reflect a lot about Leonard and how he was behaving around the phone. Thinking back about the night he rolled in at 7.00am things just did not add up when I questioned him about where he had gone. My gut instinct started talking to me; I did not like what it was saying. So one night I decided that I would wake up in the middle of the night and take a sneak into his phone, I thought I was going to shit myself, I was that scared. I managed to get his phone, snuck downstairs and started to look at his caller list. I had difficulty trying to work his Samsung phone and my hands were shaking like a leaf. I looked at some of his text messages and one of them stood out like a sore thumb even though not much was said. The text read 'Goodnight' and it was sent by... no name just the letter G. So I took that number down as well as a couple of others. I was so nervous that I actually called one of the numbers by mistake, which luckily happened to be mine, which woke Leonard up and he noticed that his phone had gone...

I started to panic, he went to the loo first then started shouting out as to what I was doing with his blood claart phone, I managed to hide the numbers I had noted down and told him exactly what I was doing. I was not satisfied with the answers that he gave me as to his whereabouts that Friday night and I suspected he was seeing someone. He denied it and I asked him about a couple of the numbers and he even said I could call them and see that they were just his friends. I continued to question him and he became very threatening in his tone so I stopped and we went back to bed.

In the morning it was as if nothing had happened, we travelled to work together as usual, and I disembarked off the train at West Ham and walked towards the jubilee line to get to Canary Wharf. On the tube my stomach was churning around, I felt nauseous and anxious; I could not wait to get off the tube. Once I was outside Canary Wharf station I called the one number that got me very suspicious and the conversation went like this:

"Hello, do you know Leonard?"

"Yes"

"And how do you know him?"

"We are seeing each other"

"And how long have you been seeing him?"

"About two weeks now"

"And when did you last see him?"

"Last Friday, he stayed over at my house. Who is this?"

"I am his wife"

"Oh, I did not know, he said he was single and living with his cousin"

"Was he not wearing his wedding ring?"

"No, oh I am sorry, I really did not know. Right! I won't be seeing him again, I am so sorry, I know what it's like, because I have had it done to me"

"Did anything happen?"

"Well no, we have not slept together"

"By the way, what colour are you?"

"I am white, why? What colour are you?"

"I am black, anyway, thanks, bye"

and I hung up the phone, completely in disbelief about the conversation that will haunt me for the rest of my life. Was this karma? I managed to get into work and tried holding it together, but I could not. I broke down once more and could not contain the tears. Once again I saw the office manager who was very concerned and sympathetic, and like before she put me in a taxi and sent me home. I cried all the way home in the taxi and I could see that the driver was very concerned for me and asked me if I was alright.

Once I got home I called Marcia and she came round in a jiffy. She asked me what I wanted to do and I said, "I want him out!" It was definitely over now. So I went upstairs and packed all his stuff. I don't where I got the energy from, maybe it was the vodka. All his stuff went into two large suitcases and about nine black bags all waiting patiently in the hallway for him to take. Marcia and I then went down Green Street to get a new lock for the door and together we changed it. I was absolutely sure that this was the end; I could not believe what he had done after everything we had been through and all I had done for him. I was just furious. I was hurting real bad. The vodka was a god send.

I called his cousin Tommy and asked him if he would be able to put up Leonard, and he wanted to know what was going on. I told him what I had not long found out, and he was surprised but said something which indicated that he knew something of this girl. He told me that I should try and work things out with Leonard, but whatever happens he would always be there for me, at that he gave the phone to Leonard, as they were working together.

I shouted down the phone and told him that he was not allowed back in this house, he could come and pick up his stuff and that it was over. I told him he could go and stay with his fancy woman. He tried to deny everything and said nothing happened, but I did not want to hear anything he had to say. He told me to wait until he came home and he would explain everything.

By the time he turned up trying to get in with his now dud key, Marcia, Troy and his fiancé Tracy, Shane and Kasima and Jennifer were all sitting in the kitchen supporting me through this terrible ordeal. I was very grateful to have my friends and family around me. Leonard was awfully embarrassed when he turned up and a small part of me felt sorry for him, but I was not about to change my mind. He had nowhere to go, and I felt a little responsible for him. My cousin Babs had called me for something and I told her what had happened. She offered to put him up for one night only until he sorted himself out.

The following day he called my grandmother (my dad's mum) and told her that he was sorry for what he had done to me and how he disrespected the family and told her how I had kicked him out and he had nowhere to go. She felt sorry for him and told him that he could stay with her until he found somewhere – he ended up staying for a year!

The following two weeks were interesting to say the least. I could not believe that I had another failed marriage. What was wrong with me? Why couldn't I get it right? I attended another meeting that David had suggested and still finding it impossible to eat only three times a day and give up sugar and white flour completely, although I made a good attempt. I felt like such a failure and realised how much I was addicted to food and sugar. David suggested that I go into rehab to help me with my addiction. Shocked at the idea I said "Do I really need to go into rehab just for food addiction?" He responded "I would not suggest it otherwise." So he started making arrangements for me to be admitted into The Priory, North London, where he also worked part time. Luckily due to the medical cover I had through work I was able to go. I just had to wait for everything to be processed. In the meantime I was suffering.

I met up with my friend Michelle for a long overdue catch up and we went to Pizza Express in Stratford. I always enjoyed meeting up with Michelle, a very sweet long-time friend of mine whom I did bible studies with when she was 17, she, however, did not come into the religion, smart move. She is actually Shane's best friend. We ordered our pizza and a glass of Shiraz each. I filled her in about my recent breakup and how I was due to go into rehab, the conversation developed and before long we were talking about how awful men could be. We decided to order a bottle of wine as it was cheaper than buying glasses. By the end of the evening we were both feeling quite tipsy, Michelle stopped drinking and I carried on making sure I finished the bottle. We then made our way home from Stratford. The following morning I got up got ready for work, and left before the kids had to go to school. I opened the front door and saw my keys in the lock. I was shocked and asked the kids if anyone had gone out this morning. But they hadn't and Adrian said, "Maybe you left them in there last night." And to my horror, he was right! I felt so bad, but pretended as if it was not a big deal.

That weekend I attended my brother Troy's wedding. It was a very small affair with just close family members at the Barkingside registry office. I was glad to be going, as it was a good distraction from what was going on in my life. My kids were at their dad's and I went with my mother. Troy was late for his own wedding because he picked up Shane. Tracy was very nervous and worried that Troy was not going to turn up. The ceremony was lovely, and they seemed so in love. I was very pleased for them and got very emotional, so much so that I sobbed like a baby not long after the ceremony. My mum hugged me and told me I would be ok; I could see the sadness, worry and care in my family's eyes. I did not want to spoil their day and managed to hold it together. We all went to a nearby restaurant for the reception. They wanted a very low key wedding and it was nice.

The wedding finished early and that night I went clubbing with Jennifer and her sister Wendy. It was a dance at the Green Light in Bow, Ronnie and Elaine had organised it as he was the DJ for the night whilst Elaine ran the bar, which suited me just fine. I had a good night out, I wanted to make sure that I enjoyed myself as much as I could seeing as I would be out of action in the Priory for a while. So in true Yvonne style I drank loads and danced hard. I pretended that I was a happy person who had not just split up with her husband of nearly four years and about to go into a psychiatric hospital.

Chapter 46

The Priory

I was due to be admitted into the Priory on the 20th February 2007, but did not go until the 22nd and in that time I became very anxious and broke down because my insurance had not been sorted out in time. I could not believe how much I was crying and called David and told him how I could not stop crying. He told me that it was good, and I was just experiencing feelings. I thought he was being quite glib and told him he was to blame for my tears, he found it quite funny.

I had asked the kids' dad if he could have them and he refused, saying that he had plans, I was horrified and told him, I was not going away for fun but going into hospital and could he not change his plans. But he did not budge on his decision. I asked my mum if she could have them, and to my surprise she agreed. She stayed over at my house so it was less disruption for them. I was ever so grateful and relieved; it made things a lot easier for me and the kids by her staying over. Finally the day came for me to go into The Priory, and I packed my suitcase and drove myself there. As I drove down the A406 I became extremely anxious. I saw the signs for the Priory and drove up the long pathway leading to the hospital. The grounds were large and it was posh, did not look like a hospital at all, more like a hotel. I checked myself in and they took me to my room which resembled a hotel room with my own en-suite bathroom. I was very impressed, and wanted to know where the gym was, but to my disappointment there was no gym. Apparently people would use the gym to exercise excessively in order to suppress their feelings; I had never heard that before!

I unpacked some of my clothes and then went to have lunch. As I sat at the table eating, I noticed the puddings and they had apple crumble, I desperately wanted to have it but thought maybe I should not because I was there to deal with my food addiction. Besides, I was sure someone was spying on me to make sure I did not indulge. I obsessed over that crumble and to this day I think about how I could have got away with having it.

I was asked some questions by a nurse, "Do you drink?" to which I replied, "I binge drink, but I don't drink every day." I did not want to answer that question; I was there for food addiction not drink problems. I wanted to be able to carry on drinking, boy did I have problems! I was given loads of books and a welcome pack.

I was thrown into a group with other addicts of sorts and was petrified. I had to fill in a questionnaire as honestly as I could and it asked all sorts of questions about my behaviour around, food, cigarettes, alcohol, relationships, drugs, gambling and sex. When I got my results back I was informed that I had issues with food, co-dependency, cigarettes, sex and alcohol. I did not want to see alcohol on there, because I had no intention of giving it up. My issue was food! I was told that if I did not have a problem with alcohol then it would not be an issue giving it up, which did not make any sense to me at that moment in time. I was not completely honest with the answers I gave around alcohol and yet it still came up that I had a problem; I however, did not want to admit that I had an addiction to alcohol.

I was weighed every morning but was not allowed to see how much I weighed. I was given plated meals, (no sugar, and no white flour) and at first I did not mind. I was allowed to choose my breakfast, and salad to accompany my meal and was given fruit salad for dessert. Other addicts were allowed to choose their meals and dessert. The group sessions were weird in the beginning, I found it hard to open up and talk, because when I did open my mouth I would get tongue tied or just start crying. At first I felt that I did not belong in the group with everyone else who abused drugs and alcohol; I was black and my issue was food; denial is a powerful thing. I saw my psychiatrist once or twice a week and he asked me how I was getting on, I did not have much to say. He told me that he felt there was a deep well of feelings inside of me that needed to come out. I did not know what he was talking about, but just cried.

As time went on I started to feel a little more comfortable in group sessions and tried to contribute, on one occasion I started to talk and subsequently broke down in tears, I actually felt traumatised and you could cut the atmosphere with a knife as I tried to get the words out. This was the beginning of the profuse crying; I did not know what was happening to me. This was about ten days into the program when all the sugar had come out of my system. I felt as raw as could be. I started talking about some of my childhood trauma, confused that they were still bothering me even though I had psychotherapy already and had explored it then. I was informed that it was not as effective as it could have been because the food and sugar was still blocking some of my feelings.

Things started to slowly make sense and I used my time there as best I could. On one occasion we had a group session they called 'family of origin.' I sat and listened to the person read out the trauma they had gone through as a child and watched as the therapist helped them rid themselves of the trauma. The atmosphere was tense and I found it so painful to listen to that I took myself out of the room, not literally but metaphorically. It was apparent by my body language – I had turned my body out of the circle and when the session was coming to an end I was asked if I identified with anything I had heard, it took a while for me to gain focus. I had identified with nearly everything and found it almost impossible to handle. After that group I ran to my bedroom and curled up into the foetal position and bawled like a baby for what seemed like eternity. I felt I was losing control of myself. Someone heard me crying and informed one of the nurses who came in and tried to console me and encouraged me not to lock myself away but to go and talk to my peers.

After two weeks my insurance would not pay for me to stay as an inpatient any longer. They would only fund me as an outpatient for a few days and then one to one therapy sessions with David. I was mortified, I was getting somewhere with the work I was doing. I had even admitted that I also had a problem with alcohol and agreed that I would give up drinking, under duress, I might add. I knew that this would not be enough as I needed more help, so I decided to pay for an extra week myself. I used two of my credit cards and split the cost of a week between the two cards, £2,000 each! For once in my life I felt I was worth it.

Night time was very scary for me and I had to sleep with the light on. One night, I felt quite restless and suddenly I woke up, someone was entering my room, I could see them approach my bed, I was petrified, I could not make out who it was. When they arrived at my bed they proceeded to take my covers off. I leapt out of my bed terrified and ran to the nurses' station and told them that someone had come into my room. They reassured me that no-one had come into my room and that I was completely safe there. I felt I was surely going mad, and feared going to sleep. Another night a dark figure was standing by my door staring at me, yep I was going mad.

I explored my own 'family of origin' trauma and looked at how my step dad treated me, how I felt I was not protected by my mother and how my own father was not around for me as I was growing up. My body had held onto all those feelings and trauma and with the help of the therapist I was able to expel a lot of my trauma.

Whilst I was in there I really started missing Leonard and although I had told the staff that I did not want calls from him I changed my mind and managed to get a message to him through Natalie to call me. But he could not get through, they had barred his number from getting through and as we were not allowed our mobiles there was no way of me speaking to him. So with my cunning self I called Natalie on her house phone and asked her to call Leonard on her mobile and she put her two phones close together so that we could speak. I cannot remember the conversation, but I arranged for him to come up and see me in order that we could have a conjoint therapy session together. Nevertheless, when he arrived a few days later I was not happy to see him and the session did not turn out as I had expected, to be honest I did not know what I expected, but by the end of it I was sure that I did not want him back. With that information I was advised not to have any contact with him.

I started to feel a lot better and although my time came for me to leave, I felt uneasy about leaving the safety blanket of The Priory. I felt so protected and I had made friends with some of the other patients. In fact there were times when we had some good belly laughs and I will never forget my experience there, it was truly an eye opener and I did an immense amount of healing. I exchanged numbers with some of my peers and was looking forward to meeting up with them at meetings. My smoking had increased, but at least my eating was under control and I had stopped drinking. I also started losing weight which was great.

Chapter 47

Home Again

Going home was daunting because I did not feel like I would be able to cope with the outside world. However, it was fine; I took things easy and still attended The Priory as a day patient to finish off my 'family of origin' work. Each day I felt a little stronger. I told the children that I was no longer able to drink either, and my daughter replied, "I knew you were alcoholic." I was shocked and ashamed to hear those words coming from my child's mouth. Who was I trying to fool all those years?

I bought my mum a gift and a card thanking her for looking after the children. I continued to work on myself and did my best to take care of my children. They themselves had been a little traumatised and unsettled by what was going on, but they were very understanding and supportive. I told them as much as they needed to know and how I would not be bringing any 'bad foods' into the house to help me. They did not mind and still don't.

I went back to work gradually under the care of the occupational health doctor. I felt overwhelmed being back at work, although it was good to be back. It was good to see people like, Lorraine, Dominic, Reena, Kate and Mark, people who really cared for me and were happy to see me back. However, it was short lived. I felt under pressure to return to work full time and then having my job description change once Mark had left the firm which I was very sad about. It did not feel right and I felt the stress building up, I went to see my GP and told her everything that had happened to me and where I had been. She signed me off work again. I did not return to work again, under the advice of David who said, "Yvonne, do not allow them to bully you, stand up for yourself." I asked for a compromise agreement, which I received. I never would have had the courage to ask for that before and I was overjoyed to have it now.

As time went on I managed to get myself a sponsor to help me in my recovery, he was actually someone that David recommended; a guy called George. David said I reminded him of George; his description was that George was the male version of me. When I first met him we were just friends and he seemed so calm and peaceful and he loved his aromatherapy oils. Before long I asked him to be my sponsor and I was very glad that I did, he took me through the 12 steps. He helped me to make crucial decisions, he listened to me cry down the phone, shout down the phone and laugh too. I learned a lot from him, he gave me unconditional love and he went beyond the call of duty and eventually became my friend.

Chapter 48

More work to do – 2009

I managed to go down three dress sizes to a size 14. I could not believe that this simple way of eating and going to my meetings was working; this was the only thing that had worked for me. No more eating on my emotions but just to fuel my body; it has not been perfect but far better than it ever has been. However, it was not just about the food, it never was, I was emotionally stunted, and was informed that when I entered rehab my emotional age was just six years old. I also had a spiritual problem which by following the twelve step program helped me to become spiritually balanced and filled that gaping hole in the pit of my stomach.

However, David kept telling me that I would feel vulnerable the smaller I became. I thought he was talking rubbish, surely I would feel happy and confident that I was now a lot slimmer, but he was right. I started receiving a lot of attention from members of the opposite sex; I could not handle it, and felt exposed and naked. I no longer had the excess fat to protect me so I would curse in my head, "They are fucking perverts," and just hated it. Needless to say I somehow sabotaged my weight loss and my meals became a little larger, and I would have a little snack here and a little snack there.

Things felt like they were going pear shaped. I started dreaming something quite disturbing; my dreams contained the same theme as the flashbacks I also started to experience; me being molested as a baby. I was speaking to a friend, Sonia on the phone about guys staring at me. I was expressing my anger calling them all perverts. I hated them staring, it wasn't so bad if I was dressed up and socialising, I half expected it. However, when I least expected it, I hated it; I wanted to do my shopping in peace. She asked me, "Why can't you be caught off guard?" Those words triggered something in me and I broke down, crying profusely. My friend was very understanding and allowed me to cry out some pain. One day on the tube I was squashed amongst a load of men, I had a panic attack, my breathing quickened, my heart started beating faster and faster and I started to sweat. I did not want to cause a scene so I managed to muster up the strength to calm myself down by taking control of my breathing. What the fuck what happening to me now, surely I had sorted out all my issues? All these incidents systematically in the space of two weeks triggered post-traumatic stress in me. I could not stop crying and felt extraordinarily scared and vulnerable. I was also having anxiety attacks; my body was tensing up especially in my sleep. I would wake up with jaw ache and pains in my arms. These experiences were extremely upsetting for me and I went to see my GP to be referred for more therapy. The distress I was feeling made me think I was going mad and at times I felt I could not go on with my life, but I never gave up hope.

I had a phone assessment for my therapy; I actually could not believe that I still needed more. 'Was I really that fucked up? If so? Why?' I thought. Whilst on the phone in my bedroom I answered the questions put to me. It lasted an hour and by the time I had finished the conversation I was literally on the floor all rolled up and in tears, the emotional pain just too much to bear. I had to wait three months before I was assigned a therapist. They suggested I see one for about six months to work more around my food issues, again another man who used cognitive behavioural therapy (CBT) to help me address my food issues. I had to fill in food journals and at times I found the sessions irritating because I needed to focus on my abuse issues. However, it was arranged that I would have women's group therapy after to deal with that. In the meantime I continually attended my meetings which were a great support for me as well as my sponsor and friends.

My stepfather was now living in Dominica. I heard that he went into a coma autumn 2009; I found it very hard to deal with, I wasn't upset because he was ill, I was upset because I needed to confront him, so I wrote a letter expressing my anger, pain, sadness and disgust for him. A week later my aunty texted me that he had died and could I pass the message onto my brothers. I was vexed, not because he had died but because I was on my way out with the girls and receiving this news was really bad timing. I forwarded the text to my brothers and pushed it to the back of my mind. However, by the end of the night it triggered me into a frenzied state. I was livid that I did not send him the letter or even get to confront him. My brother Troy did not go to his own dads' funeral on account of me. He offered a listening ear and showed me loads of compassion – God bless him.

Once I had completed my six months with my CBT therapist I waited a couple months for my space to become available at the women's group therapy. I was very apprehensive about attending, but also felt it was about time that my space had come up. I did not want to waste much time. I wanted to heal;

however, my first few weeks were daunting. I was not sure if I could trust these women, they were strangers to me. Listening to their experiences somehow helped me to start relaxing and trusting. They all had similar experiences. I started to open up and I spoke about my life and my journey thus far. I felt I had a bit of a head start due to my time at the Priory. As the weeks went by I was talking more and crying lots. I started to feel angry; it was as if I had all this anger inside me that I did not know about, it felt like a big red hot ball inside my abdomen. It needed to come out. There was also a lot of sadness inside, a feeling of acute sadness whereby the only way I could express it was to cry like a baby, as words were not enough. Due to no more medicating on food and sugar I had what therapists call recovered memory; the sexual abuse had started at the pre-verbal stage when I was a baby by my stepfather. I had blocked it out for 40 years and now it was killing me. It felt like it had just happened and the baby in me was suffering and needed healing.

Realising that I had been tampered with at such a tender age and not just the one occurrence I remembered at the age of six has made me feel extremely angry and so incredibly sad for the little girl in me. Sometimes I wonder how I survived at the hands of my stepfather, he abused me sexually, mentally and emotionally. No wonder I wanted to block it all out. However, better out than in, so I continued to express my anger, guilt, sadness, pain and shame in my sessions.

I am amazed at how the human body can block out such traumatic events and doubly amazed at how I am slowly being healed emotionally from these traumas just by not using food, alcohol, men and behaviours to suppress them. I have faith that

God will give me the courage to continue trusting that I will be ok.

Chapter 49

Studies

When I gave up my job at Morgan Stanley, I knew I had to retrain. I felt confident enough now to try something different. I enrolled at my local college to do an Access course, equivalent to 'A' levels. There was a preliminary test I had to do which I did and felt confident enough. A week later I received my results and had passed. I chose my main subjects psychology and sociology. I enjoyed studying, and I was a star pupil. I liked my main subjects as I found them interesting although I had to do maths as part of the course, which did not please me in the slightest. Karen, who I became good friends with, once asked me if I wanted some camomile tea in the middle of a maths class. I was perplexed as to why she would ask me such an irrelevant question. It turned out that Karen could see me becoming somewhat irate in class due to what I thought was the teacher's incompetence. Oh how I hated maths.

Despite this I progressed well throughout the course and even passed my maths after receiving a lesson from Karen's boyfriend who assured me that I knew my stuff and just needed to believe in myself. Our final assignment was that of a 6,000 word essay. I chose to do it on the subject of addiction. It was a subject close to my heart and I felt I knew enough about it and would enjoy finding out even more. My tutor Iona advised me that I would need to be careful to not be biased. Karen and I got on well with this particular tutor and I told her a little bit about my life. I got stuck into my essay doing loads of research and finally handed it in. When Iona handed it back she told me that I was an excellent writer and encouraged me to publish my essay. I was chuffed; I had discovered a new talent! I also won an iPod from the college for receiving top marks as the best student all round in my group. I then decided I would put my talent to use; so many people had told me I was inspiring so I starting writing this book. I left it for a while and in order to spur me on my brothers Shane and Troy bought me a laptop for my 40th birthday.

I wanted to continue my studies and do a degree in Addiction Therapy. The only one that appealed to me was a two year Masters' degree and even though I had no prior degree, I was still accepted on the course. However, I could not find funding and could not afford to pay for the course and it was too late to find another counselling course so I decided to do an online life coaching course. I was thrilled with life coaching, I started to implement the new techniques for myself i.e. how to make goals and how to achieve them. I started reading loads of self-help and spiritual books and continued to grow and develop myself.

In the meantime I managed to find a counselling degree that I wanted to do starting in Sept 2009. Luckily for me it was at my local college in the new university campus. I organised my student loan and was excited about finally being able to study at degree level, something I never thought I was able to do. I sailed through my first year of university. I loved every minute of it. Yes it was a little challenging, but it was a subject I enjoyed and I felt as if I was thriving. My grades were excellent, a few B's and even more A's. My second year was more challenging and I felt extremely stressed in the second semester. Despite this I managed to get straight A's for all my modules.

I attended a free event called Breakthrough to Success run by Christopher Howard a successful American Life Coach; they use hypnosis, subconscious reprogramming and NLP. I had an amazing time and it was all a part of my growth. The following year I attended again and was fortunate enough to win one of the prizes, a course worth £5,000. On this course I dealt with even more issues. I went through a process on the stage called Parts Integration where, with the assistance of the course leader I integrated Yvonne the scared baby, Yvonne the sad little girl, Yvonne the angry teenager and Yvonne the mature adult. It was a mind blowing experience that was so powerful everyone in the audience was in awe of how I looked the following day. I felt lighter and looked like I had let go of more trauma and was definitely seeing the world with new eyes. I also learned techniques to add to my life coaching skills. My life was coming together and I was excited. By now I was finally divorced, I had waited far too long to file for it and now it had come through, I started to feel free.

Chapter 50

Sweet Love - 2010

Three years had passed and I had been without a man, well I had a couple of escapades but they did not work out. I was tired of still attracting the wrong sort and was glad I had decided to take time out and work on myself so that I would be in a better position to attract the right sort. I was still clubbing occasionally and at first found it a little scary as I often felt quite vulnerable, but after time I started to become a lot more comfortable. I realised that I needed to stop talking about men in such a derogatory way. Yes, most of the men in my life had fucked me up in one way or the other, but I needed to realise that not all men were dogs and I then made a very conscious decision to stop the negative talk about men and not long after that's when it happened...

One night at the IF Bar in Ilford I was out with Elaine, her husband Ronnie was DJ-ing there. I was happy to be out as I had not been out in a little while. I was certainly used to going out now without drinking, my confidence was fine and I did not miss the drink in the slightest. I was ready to boogie the night away and then there was an announcement that we were to be entertained by an R&B singer. I was a little put out, I wanted to get my groove on, not listen to someone sing. I did not pay much attention as the singer came on the stage, I did not even hear his name. I became a little impatient and decided to go to the toilet to pass the time.

On my return he was still on stage about to sing his second song. I was not amused. Then I decided to pay attention, I had no choice really. As I looked up, I saw him properly for the first time, my heart jumped slightly, he looked like he did body building, his hair was in cornrow and he was casually dressed. I said to Elaine, "Ooh, he's nice." Elaine responded, "Oh, I know him, I used to go to school with him, his name is Sean." Sean was asking for a single woman to come up on stage whilst he sang his second song. No-one budged. I looked at him more closely he smiled such a sweet smile and something told me to go on stage, but I was stuck. Then he opened up his shirt slightly and before I knew it a force of power walked me up onto the stage.

The audience clapped and as I arrived in front of him, I wanted to turn back around and run off the stage. I whispered to him, "What shall I do?" He responded, "Just dance whilst I sing." So there I was dancing on stage with a complete stranger singing 'A house is not a home' by Luther Vandross. He sang it well, he was doing the whole performing bit, going on his knees and singing to me. I felt special but painfully shy too. What happened to Yvonne the performer? He held me tenderly and then whispered in my ear "You feel nice." "Behave yourself," I replied. The song went on for ages and all eyes were on me, I found it a little daunting. Finally the song finished and he thanked me nicely and handed me one of his CD's.

Half an hour later, Sean was in front of me asking me why I was single. I told him in no uncertain terms, "Because I cannot find a man on my level." He then asked me, "So what kind of man are you looking for?" I abruptly responded with, "A man that is loyal, ambitious, loving, spiritual, caring, into personal development and fun." He proceeded to ask me, "Do you have all those qualities?" I said, "Of course." Sean then said, "Would you like to come outside for a chat?" We went outside and spoke for 25 minutes in the freezing cold. It was March 2010. The rest is history.

Sean and I exchanged numbers, he said he would call me, two weeks passed and I had not heard from him. I became very angry, I could not believe that I had met a man that ticked all the right boxes and he did not call me. I was given some advice to just call him because maybe he had lost his phone or my number. I decided to call him and he had lost my number and was so glad that I had called him. We had a chat and arranged to meet up in a couple of days. Our first date was fun, we went to the Stratford Circus bar and then onto Zazas for a little boogie. He was lovely, a single father looking after his two teenage girls living in Goodmayes. He was a school teacher and running his own supplementary school. I was impressed. At the end of the date, we kissed goodbye, it was a soft and tender kiss and I felt the sparks, I had a good feeling about this one.

We saw each other fairly often and by the end of April we had decided to become an item. I was happy with my new man. Some of my issues threw themselves into the relationship. I felt it was necessary to inform Sean of my past due to some of my weird behaviours. I told him that I had been sexually abused and how I had been to rehab etc etc, as I told him this I cried, finding it difficult to be vulnerable and expose myself. Sean responded with holding me close kissing my tears and calling me his amazing girl. I knew I had found a gem in Sean.

Being single and strong was easy, being strong whilst in a relationship is challenging, and that's when my real strength of character showed. We have worked hard at our relationship, we both recognise that we sometimes try to sabotage the good thing that we have and we work together to solve our problems. Sean communicates more than me and makes me feel safe and secure within the relationship. He has helped me to have more respect for myself as a woman, by showing me respect. I have never been with such an understanding and loving man and our love continues to grow and deepen. We plan to buy a home together next year.

Sean is also very passionate about personal development, which really excites me. He has attended some of the personal development seminars with me and it's great that we have this in common. We have created a relationship workshop together and have delivered it a few times. Our plan is to develop it and create others so that we can help couples to have healthy loving relationships whilst we also continue to perfect ours.

Chapter 51

And Now? 2011

My self-esteem is building; I was shocked at how low my self-esteem actually was. The confidence I had portrayed was not real, it was misplaced. I have found out that I am not the person I always portrayed, bubbly, life and soul of the party. There is a part of me that can be quite shy, but that's ok. I am in touch with the real me and I continue to work on liking who I am. I am connecting more to the spiritual part of me and starting to feel whole and at peace and it's the best feeling ever. Sometimes I have moments of true serenity and it is amazing, I never thought I would ever feel like this. Yes life still happens and shit happens too, but I have different coping mechanisms which work far better than shoving food down my mouth or drinking alcohol or relying on a man to fix me, (although I still sometimes struggle with the food). Acceptance is the key – this is a very valuable statement and it takes away so many struggles and discomfort when I learn to accept people, places and things and going with the flow of life.

I am also discovering new talents, one of which you are hopefully enjoying now – writing. That's what inspired me to write this book I want to reach out to those of you out there who may relate to my story and know that there is help out there. Secrets kept me sick, there is no need to keep my secrets hidden away, they kept me sick for 40 years, and I am one of millions who has been through shit and I have nothing to be ashamed of. I no longer need to hold onto the shame, guilt, anger and fear, it is damaging to my serenity and my progress.

My relationship with my children is far better than it ever was, I am now more emotionally present for them and they notice the difference. They are doing well emotionally and academically, I am so grateful to them for showing me understanding and giving me unconditional love. I also have mended the relationship I have with my mother. She also has gone through her journey and explored her issues, in a different way to myself, nonetheless it has helped us bond and I can now truly say that I love my mother dearly, she is a lot stronger than I thought she was. I speak to my dad a couple of times a year and for now that's fine for me as I accept him the way he is. I truly have forgiven my sister for what happened. In fact I have forgiven everyone for the wrongs they did me and am sorry for the wrongs I did them also.

June 2009 I started my work placement in a rehab called Kairos in South London; I trained as an Addiction therapist and learned a great deal. I met some lovely people who taught me a lot and showed me love and patience and I am grateful for their belief and faith in my abilities. I was seeing another counsellor/life coach to help me move forward and along with the courses I moved on from Kairos in January 2011 and decided to become self employed as a life coach and counsellor, and it has been challenging. My business is still in the early stages and it excites me that I am finally fulfilling my purpose and look forward to helping many people on their journey to self-discovery. I met a wonderful woman called Sandra at women's group therapy who showed me great empathy, she was an angel. We have become good friends and business partners in a project that we have put together with another great friend I met a few years back called Paula. I met Paula at a christening 4 years ago through Natalie and we instantly got on at a very deep level – people come into our life for a reason, season or lifetime! Together we are building our project to help women who suffer from mild to moderate depression and social phobias. We are very excited.

I have not had a drink since 19th February 2007! On the 19th June 2010 I finally won the battle to the dreaded cigarette! I am free from nicotine addiction. Yes I did put on some weight and I continue to work on that aspect of my life.

In October 2011 I decided to go on a seven day fast with Sean. It took quite a while for him to convince me to do this, I had never been without food, in fact the thought of being without food sent me into a bit of a panic. However, after much deliberation and spiritual preparation I made the decision to join him. It was very challenging; all we had was water and herbal teas. At times I felt I was going to faint. How did I cope? I kept praying, drinking and joking; joking around a bit made the time go by quickly. Days three and four were very challenging, nonetheless I got through it, Sean was a great support and so were my friends and children.

By the time I finished the fast I was over the moon, it was nothing short of a miracle. I did it! I went seven days without food, a woman who relied on food for all her life. I felt empowered and it was then that the phrase, 'you can do whatever it is you put your mind to,' really came alive for me. I lost some much needed weight and it kick started me back into healthy eating and weight loss. I am definitely back on the right track and really feel ready to let the slim me out of her shell without feeling vulnerable.

Chapter 52

Lessons Learnt

When I look back at my life now and what I have learned about myself as someone with addictive tendencies, it all seems to make sense. I started overeating as a child in order to block out the pain of my childhood and because of the messages I received from my stepdad. Sugar was a powerful aid in doing this and I only realised how powerful when I managed to stop using sugar. It worked just like a drug for me. Compulsive overeating is just as serious as anorexia and bulimia, which I had no idea of and in fact my overeating often turned into a form of bulimia whereby I tried to get rid of the excess food by abusing laxatives and over-exercising.

I became emotionally attached to men very quickly, sometimes almost instantly which was me being either co-dependent or becoming addicted to love and in essence loving the fantasy and taking me away from reality. The attempted suicides were due to my love addiction, not having enough self-esteem to feel 'enough' by myself. I tried to control my men, which again is another addictive behaviour, at the time I knew no other way. Intimacy was very difficult for me and even now it is something that I am constantly working on.

I can see how easy it is for me to cross addict switching from food to alcohol, and food to cigarettes – I would use people, places and things to avoid my feelings at any cost. When I stopped using these things I would and still have intense feelings and need to have the courage to let them flow through me and express them. Being someone with addictive tendencies having such deep feelings has its upside; it means I feel the good feelings just as powerfully. I am a sensitive soul and I see this as a gift. Having this knowledge has made a big impact on my life because I now know why I did the things I did. I now know who I am.

I have an awareness of self, second to none now. I know when I am trying to run away from my feelings. I know when I am feeling fearful, anxious, vulnerable, angry, lonely, happy, sad, overwhelmed, bored etc etc. Before rehab my feelings were just happy, sad, excited or depressed. It has been a task and a half getting in touch with my feelings and learning how to express them in an appropriate manner and learning to just accept that it is all a part of life and that to be human means to feel. For me, being vulnerable was very frightening, because for me it meant I would get hurt in some way or other, or be taken advantage of. However, being vulnerable now is actually ok; I have enough in my emotional bank to know who to trust with my vulnerability. And again, it is acceptable to be vulnerable; it's part of being human.

I have dreams and goals that I know I can achieve now; I always wanted to get that degree and now finally I am studying and I can see that certificate. My journey has not been easy, in fact going into rehab and living in recovery has been the hardest thing I have ever had to do. I had to fundamentally reprogram my mind and change all my core belief systems; however that has led me to meet the real me for which I will be eternally grateful. And I love me! I do believe that people came into my life for a reason, a season or a lifetime. The lessons I have learnt are very valuable to me.

What has not killed me has certainly made me stronger! I no longer survive, I live.

You can transform your life as long as you're breathing.

About The Author

Yvonne J Douglas' purpose and passion is to inspire, empower and motivate individuals to reach their highest potential. She does this through her counselling, personal development coaching, writing, inspirational speaking, intuitive readings and energy healing. A dynamic individual who just by her aura can change the people she comes into contact with. Yvonne is the proud mother of two young adults, whom she brought up on her own, guiding and encouraging them to take charge of their lives.

Yvonne has become an extremely empowered individual due to her tenacity, courage and determination to heal herself. She is dedicated in helping others heal from past hurts, pain and traumas.

Yvonne's private practice aims to provide an exemplary service to enable individuals to face their fears and release their emotional baggage in order to become the success they have always dreamt of. Yvonne prides herself in making people successful in all areas of life and endeavours to lead by example.

Issues that Yvonne can help with in her counselling practice include addictions, phobias, anxiety, depression, trauma, sexual abuse, emotional issues, and low self-esteem and relationship problems. Her personal development coaching includes one to one coaching as well as workshops which will obliterate negative core beliefs, trauma and the like, moving you through change enabling you to tap into your most powerful self and achieving magnificent results.

Yvonne has been recognised by Worldwide Who's Who for her counselling achievements in November 2011. In July 2012 Yvonne was chosen as an inspirational figure within the Black 100+ legacy book, in addition, she was selected as one of the top 50 inspirational and international people by the Swanilenga Group Ltd. She has been on numerous radio shows talking about her experiences and her book. Yvonne has started writing her second book entitled Your Protection, Your Guide, Trust Your Intuition, which promises to be an illuminating and empowering read; she plans to go global with her public speaking as she is currently one of the most inspirational speakers in the UK. For more information on Yvonne please visit www.yvonnejdouglas.com.

26747079R00163

Made in the USA
Columbia, SC
19 September 2018